MANNA

MANNA

Food For The Soul (Volume 2)

ZIRI DAFRANCHI

Heredita Press Limited

A CIP catalogue record is available from the British Library.
Ebook ISBN: 978-1-7398021-1-0
Paperback ISBN: 978-1-7398021-2-7

Hereditas Press
www.hereditaspress.com

BODY AND SOUL

*As our bodies need daily nourishment to thrive, so do
our spirits require daily nourishment to truly thrive
and to remain actively alive.
The food of the spirit is the Word of God.*

Contents

DEVOTIONALS

Preface

In the busy world of today, with many things demanding for our attention from the moment we open our eyes in bed each morning, it has become easy for us misplacing our priorities. It is now common practice for many people to reach for their mobile phones first thing after waking up each morning even while still in bed. Social media seems to have become a god of sorts in this generation as more and more people get sucked into its allures. Each day, we are inundated with an overwhelming amount of notifications on WhatsApp, Facebook, Twitter, LinkedIn, Instagram, TikTok, Pinterest, and other social media platforms we are subscribed to, from the moment we wake up in the morning throughout the day up until the moment we drift off to sleep at the end of the day. Consequently, social media takes up a significant portion of our time each day to the detriment of other more important things we are meant to accomplish on a given day.

Research has shown that the first ten minutes of each day are the most crucial, further revealing that "scrolling through emails or checking social media wasn't the best start of the day because it puts us in the reactive rather than proactive seat." Starting each day wrongly could be more detrimental to us in many other ways apart from simply ruining that day. A wrong or bad day could result in a bad week which could result in a bad month and ultimately in a bad year. Life, however, is too short such that every single second is precious. To maximise every moment, we need to start our day right!

There could be no better way to start our day right than spending quality time feeding our soul with spiritual food—Manna. A healthy soul makes for a better life. Sadly, it would seem that we mostly look after the body while ignoring our spirits even though, ironically, without the spirit the body would cease to exist. It is thus incumbent upon all who desire a fulfilled life to ensure that our spirits are duly nourished regularly, if not daily. The nourishing of the soul is the primary purpose of the *Manna: Food For The Soul* series, which I have written not because I simply wanted to write devotional books.

Personally, I have never believed in a one-size-fits-all-type of devotional since it is unlikely that the same scriptural exhortation and meditation could apply to everyone at the same time, every day of each year. Reality shows that we are all different individuals walking different paths in life and each faced with unique experiences, meaning that on the same day a particular person is awakening to a breakthrough in an aspect of life is the very day another person is awakening to a disaster or challenge. Now it is obvious that both individuals require different types of exhortation: the former may have to give thanks and praises while the latter may have to seek for courage and strength. In the natural sense, we all eat different types of food each day in varied quantities and combination but we do not all eat the same food as everyone else every day. Sometimes we may even be required to go on a specific diet due to one reason or another. Likewise, the nourishing of our spirit should be customised to suit individual needs and not presented as a set meal for everyone regardless of what each person is going through at any given moment. This is the main reason I have never been a fan of books of daily devotionals, especially those dated for each day of a given year. And I would never have thought of writing one myself. I wrote my very first devotional sometime late in 2019 when I was requested to contribute to a devotional group, DWELLING IN THE SECRET PLACE, by the founder, Apostle Larai Aduma. This unlocked hidden potentials in me and opened me up to new inspirations. The devotionals I wrote were food to my own soul as much as they were to the souls of those who read them. It was while I continued to contribute devotionals in this group that the thought of compiling my contributions into a book was dropped in my spirit. I reasoned that it would be a blessing to more than just the members of the group.

The *Manna: Food For The Soul* series is unique and different to your usual devotional book for two main reasons: First, its contents include poetic meditations which are based on and inspired by referenced scriptural texts. Perhaps the first of its kind. Furthermore, its

devotional content is presented thematically thus enabling you to decide which devotional to read at any given time based on individual disposition and need. Its contents are more like a buffet than set meal, meaning that you are in full control how you choose to utilise them. You decide what to feast on in any given day, how much you want to eat, how you want to eat, and when you want to eat from its contents. You could meditate on more than one devotional on a particular day or you could spread a devotional over different days; you could also choose to feast on more than one devotional on a given day. As a buffet-type devotional book, it is up to you to select what goes into your menu for each day based on what your spirit hungers for thus enabling you to feast till your soul if fully satisfied.

I pray your soul is well nourished and that you find strength and encouragement from the meditations and devotionals contained in Volume 2 which includes lessons from the lives of popular biblical characters like Noah, Moses, Elijah, David, Hannah, Ruth, Gideon, Naaman, Naboth, Jabez, Jonah, Job, and many others.

I will like to express my gratitude to God for availing me with daily manna and also for the privilege of sharing with others. I am also grateful to Larai Aduma for the privilege of contributing devotionals on her platform, which has now enabled me to share *manna* with the world. Finally, I will like to acknowledge and thank Joanna Basinga and Ujunwa Ogbonna for an excellent edit, and also the staff of Hereditas Press for their excellent service.

Poetic Meditations

POETIC MEDITATIONS

I

All Is Vanity

"Vanity of vanities," says the Preacher.
"Vanity of vanities! All [that is done without God's guidance]
is vanity [futile, meaningless—a wisp of smoke,
a vapor that vanishes, merely chasing the wind]."
(Ecclesiastes 1: 2 AMP)

Every day we strive and labour
Every day we plan and take action
Every day we acquire and accumulate
As every day we try to make a living

Every day we dream and aspire
Every day we pursue our dreams
Every day we raise our ambition
As every day we try to make a living

Every day we hope for a better tomorrow
Every day we edge closer to the grave
Every day we fail to live
As every day we try to make a living

One day we will discover that
Life does not consist in our possessions
When after we die we, leave them all behind
And only then realise that all is vanity.

Reflection
*Spend some moments reflecting on the vanity
of failing to live while trying to make a living.*

2

Wealthy Place

Thou hast caused men to ride over our heads;
We went through fire and through water:
But thou broughtest us out into a wealthy place.
(Psalms 66: 12 KJV)

Great is your goodness, O Lord
Working in strange and uncertain ways
Your wonders to perform
You are perfect in all your ways

Great is your wisdom, O Lord
Using foolishness to confound the wise
And weakness to overcome the mighty
You are perfect in all your ways

Great is your faithfulness, O Lord
You tried and proved us, as by fire
Only to bring us to a wealthy place
You are perfect in all your ways.

Reflection
*Spend some moments reflecting on God's plan to bring you
to a place of abundance through your trials and tribulations.*

3

Way-Maker

Behold, I will do a new thing;
now it shall spring forth;
shall ye not know it?
I will even make a way in the wilderness,
and rivers in the desert.
(Isaiah 43: 19 KJV)

When I trust and obey
His guidance and direction
Even through the wilderness
God will make a way

When I walk the path
Where He leads me
Even where there is no way
God will make a way

When I labour in the field
Where He has called me
Even when strength fails
God will make a way

When at last I am done
And it is time to go home
Even when I know not how
God will make a way.

Reflection
*Spend some moments reflecting on God's ability
to make a way where it seems there is no way.*

4

Strength For The Weak

He giveth power to the faint;
and to them that have no might
he increaseth strength.
(Isaiah 40: 29 KJV)

Strength will rise
As I wait patiently on God
Silently seeking His face
To do what He promised

Strength will rise
As I do what He bids me
Persistently and faithfully
Despite opposition and resistance

Strength will rise
As I cling to Him
In season and out of season
Even when all else fails

Strength will rise
As I grow weary and weak
Because in my weakness
God's strength is made perfect in me.

Reflection
*Spend some moments reflecting on
the joy of the Lord as the source of your strength.*

5

Shout For Victory!

And it came to pass at the seventh time,
when the priests blew with the trumpets,
Joshua said unto the people,
Shout;
for the LORD hath given you the city.
(Joshua 6: 16 KJV)

Shout!
When the cloud over you is darkened
And problems never rain but pour
There is victory ahead

Shout!
When surrounded by many armies
And the battle is set in array
There is victory ahead

Shout!
When friends misunderstand you
And abandon and forsake you
There is victory ahead

Shout!
When your trials are endless
And you despair and are perplexed
There is victory ahead

Shout!
When you've trusted and obeyed
And there is nothing left to do
There is victory ahead.

Reflection
Are you faced with insurmountable challenges?
Faith sings in victory in the midst of battle.

6

Step-By-Step

The steps of a [good and righteous] man
are directed and established by the Lord,
And He delights in his way [and blesses his path].
(Psalms 37: 23 AMP)

Step by step God leads me
From the cradle to the grave
Through this journey called life
To accomplish His plans for me

Step by step God leads me
From the valley to the mountain
Through the changing scenes of life
To bring me to an expected end

Step by step God leads me
From sunrise to sunset
Through the many seasons of life
As I trust and obey Him.

Reflection
Are your daily steps ordered by God?

7

Strong Tower

The name of the Lord is a strong tower;
The righteous runs to it and is safe and set on high
[far above evil].
(Proverbs 18: 10 AMP)

Some trust in chariots
Some trust in horses
We trust in the name of the Lord

Some trust in riches
Some trust in wealth
We trust in the name of the Lord

Some trust in power
Some trust in might
We trust in the name of the Lord

Some trust in fame
Some trust in fortune
We trust in the name of the Lord

The name of the Lord
Is our strong tower
Where we are safe and secure.

Reflection
Where is your trust?

8

Beautiful Ending

He hath made every thing beautiful in his time:
also he hath set the world in their heart,
so that no man can find out the work that God maketh
from the beginning to the end.
(Ecclesiastes 3: 11 KJV)

All your plans, O Lord are good
You've appointed a time for every plan
When the time is right
You make everything beautiful

You set a time for me to be born
Even before my parents were born
At the appointed time I was born
You made everything beautiful

You set a time for every purpose in my life
Even before I was conceived and born
At the time appointed for each
You made everything beautiful

Although You make me wait at times
Even when I am tired of waiting
When the time is right
You make everything beautiful

Although the process is not always good
At times it looks bad, very bad
When the time is right
You make everything beautiful.

Reflection
Do not focus on how things are now.
God's plans for you are for your good.
He will eventually make everything beautiful.

9

Not My Battle

The Lord will fight for you while you
[only need to] keep silent and remain calm."
(Exodus 14: 14 AMP)

When billows roll and tempests fall
And all hell is let loose around me
I shall be calm
The Lord will fight for me

When I am troubled on every side
And persecuted in every way
I shall be calm
The Lord will fight for me

When I am misunderstood by friends
And falsely accused by family
I shall be calm
The Lord will fight for me

When I am cast down and perplexed
And darkness suddenly overshadows me
I shall be calm
The Lord will fight for me.

Reflection
Are you threatened in any way?
Hold your peace and let God fight for you.

King Of Glory

Lift up your heads, O gates,
And be lifted up, ancient doors,
That the King of glory may come in.
Who is the King of glory?
The Lord strong and mighty,
The Lord mighty in battle.
(Psalms 24: 7–8 AMP)

Be fruitful bareness and release your harvest
Long overdue and muchly deserved
The King of Glory has come
Who is the King of Glory?
The Lord of Hosts is the King of Glory

Be open ancient doors and release your treasures
Long hidden from God's anointed
The King of Glory has come
Who is the King of Glory?
The Lord of Hosts is the King of Glory

Be broken bars of iron and release your captives
Long imprisoned and in chains
The King of Glory has come
Who is the King of Glory?
The Lord of Hosts is the King of Glory

The Lord strong and mighty
The Lord mighty in battle
The Lord of hosts and Man of war
Jehovah is his name
Jehovah is the King of Glory.

Reflection
Whatever your circumstance
Let the King of Glory in.

I I

Let God Arise!

Let God arise, and His enemies be scattered;
Let those who hate Him flee before Him.
(Psalms 68: 1 AMP)

As they gather and plot
Evil conspirators united by hate
Seeking to harm or destroy
Let God arise!

As they rage and rant
Enemies driven by arrogance
Threatening fire and brimstone
Let God arise!

As they dance and rave
Enjoying and celebrating exuberantly
What they presume is my end
Let God arise!

Let God arise!
To frustrate the devices of the crafty
To confound the plans of the wicked
And scatter His enemies.

Reflection
Do not focus on the enemy or problem
Instead, pray that God will arise.

12

Man Of War

The LORD is a man of war:
The LORD is his name.
(Exodus 15: 3 KJV)

Who brought Pharaoh down to his knees?
Who turned the captivity of Israel?
Who parted the Red Sea?
The Lord, Man of war

Who brought water out from the rock?
Who rained manna from the heavens?
Who led Israel through the wilderness?
The Lord, Man of war

Who brought Israel to the promised land?
Who brought down the walls of Jericho?
Who defeated Israel's enemies?
The Lord, Man of war

Who will order my steps aright?
Who will answer when I call?
Who will fight all my battles?
The Lord, Man of war.

Reflection
With God on your side
Who can be against you?

13

Everlasting Love

The LORD hath appeared of old unto me, saying,
Yea, I have loved thee with an everlasting love:
therefore with lovingkindness have I drawn thee.
(Jeremiah 31: 3 KJV)

Your love, O Lord, never fails
From day to day, age to age
From everlasting to everlasting
It never ceases

Your mercies, O Lord, never fails
From day to day, age to age
From everlasting to everlasting
It never ceases

Your faithfulness, O Lord, never fails
From day to day, age to age
From everlasting to everlasting
It never ceases

Your kindness, O Lord, never fails
From day to day, age to age
From everlasting to everlasting
It never ceases

Your goodness, O Lord, never fails
From day to day, age to age
From everlasting to everlasting
It never ceases.

Reflection
*Spend some moments reflecting on
God's everlasting love for you.*

14

My Healer

*And said, If thou wilt diligently hearken to
the voice of the LORD thy God,
and wilt do that which is right in his sight,
and wilt give ear to his commandments,
and keep all his statutes,
I will put none of these diseases upon thee,
which I have brought upon the Egyptians:
for I am the LORD that healeth thee.*
(Exodus 15: 26 KJV)

Who restores my soul?
Who makes my mind sound?
Who heals me when I am broken?
Jehovah Rapha my healer

Who keeps me from harm?
Who protects me from danger?
Who heals all my diseases?
Jehovah Rapha my healer

Who sets the captive free?
Who delivers the oppressed?
Who heals our land?
Jehovah Rapha my healer.

Reflection
Is Jehovah Rapha your healer?

15

No Weapon!

No weapon that is formed against you will succeed;
And every tongue that rises against you
in judgment you will condemn. This
[peace, righteousness, security, and triumph over opposition]
is the heritage of the servants of the Lord,
And this is their vindication from Me," says the Lord.
(Isaiah 54: 17 AMP)

Every word spoken against me
Before any oracle or shrine
Or released in the atmosphere
Shall not prosper

Every plan devised against me
To bring me harm or shame
Or to bring me destruction
Shall not prosper

Every accusation raised against me
Before any judge or court
To bring me condemnation and guilt
Shall not prosper

Every battle waged against me
In the spiritual or natural
Known or unknown
Shall not prosper

No weapon formed against me
In any shape or size
Shall accomplish its purpose
This is my heritage in God.

Reflection
With God on your side
No weapon shall prosper against you.

16

Sing For Joy

Let the godly ones exult in glory;
Let them sing for joy on their beds.
(Psalms 149: 5 AMP)

Sing, O sing for joy
And rejoice in the Lord
Who has lifted up our strength
And enlarged our mouth over our enemies

Sing, O sing for joy
And rejoice in the Lord
Who has strengthened the weak
And broken the bows of the mighty

Sing, O sing for joy
And rejoice in the Lord
Who has satisfied the hungry
And made the arrogant-rich hungry

Sing, O sing for joy
And rejoice in the Lord
Who has given children to the barren
And made the haughty mother of many childless

Sing, O sing for joy
And rejoice in the Lord
Who has raised the poor out of the dust
And made kings and princes beggars

Sing, O sing for joy
And rejoice in the Lord
Who has turned again our captivity
And filled our tongue with singing.

Reflection
Spend some moments reflecting on God's ability
To turn your situation around.

17

My Redeemer Liveth

For I know that my redeemer liveth,
And that he shall stand
at the latter day upon the earth:
(Job 19: 25 KJV)

Accused and oppressed
Despised and forsaken
Abandoned and dejected
Still I stand
Because my Redeemer liveth

Shaken and broken
Ridiculed and Scorned
Beaten and damaged
Still I stand
Because my Redeemer liveth

Persecuted and afflicted
Reproached and shamed
Cast down and entrapped
Still I stand
Because my Redeemer liveth

Tested and tried
Chosen and approved
Refined and restored
I stand vindicated
Because my Redeemer liveth

Reflection
You will overcome
Because your Redeemer liveth.

18

Awake, Zion

Awake, awake; put on thy strength, O Zion;
put on thy beautiful garments, O Jerusalem, the holy city:
for henceforth there shall no more come into thee
the uncircumcised and the unclean.
Shake thyself from the dust; arise, and sit down, O Jerusalem:
loose thyself from the bands of thy neck, O captive daughter of Zion.
(Isaiah 52: 1–2 KJV)

Awake, awake, O Zion
Put on your beautiful garment
Your strength and righteousness
For the glory of the Lord is risen upon you

Awake, awake, O Zion
Shake yourself from the dust
Your desolation and brokenness
For the glory of the Lord is risen upon you

Awake, awake, O Zion
Break the bands off your neck
Your captivity and oppression
For the glory of the Lord is risen upon you

Awake, awake, O Zion
Put on your beautiful garment
Your strength and righteousness
For the glory of the Lord is risen upon you.

Reflection
God will turn every captivity
And restore you fully.

19

Remember God

Remember [thoughtfully] also your Creator
in the days of your youth
[for you are not your own, but His],
before the evil days come or
the years draw near when you will say
[of physical pleasures],
"I have no enjoyment and delight in them."
(Ecclesiastes 12: 1 AMP)

When you are young and full of strength
And nothing seems impossible to you
When everything is well and good
And all your dreams are realised
Remember God

When you are sad and in despair
And the world is a lonely place to be
When nothing is working to plan
And everything is going the wrong way
Remember God

When you are betrayed and disappointed
And it is hard to trust again
When you have tried your very best
And there is nothing to show for it
Remember God

When you are remembered and restored
And everything is bright again
When you are raised and lifted up
And you feel on top of the world
Remember God

When you are old and frail
And living becomes a chore
When your appointed days are over
And it is time for you to go home
Remember God.

Reflection
Whatever your circumstances
Remember God.

20

A Song Of My Beloved

Now will I sing to my wellbeloved a song of my beloved touching his vineyard. My wellbeloved hath a vineyard in a very fruitful hill: and he fenced it, and gathered out the stones thereof, and planted it with the choicest vine, and built a tower in the midst of it, and also made a winepress therein: and he looked that it should bring forth grapes, and it brought forth wild grapes.
(Isaiah 5: 1–3 KJV)

I will sing to my well-beloved
A song of my well-beloved
Who sowed precious seeds
In hope of an abundant harvest
But got thorns and briers in return

I will sing to my well-beloved
A song of my well-beloved
Who built a strong tower
For shelter and protection
But it collapsed in the storm

I will sing to my well-beloved
A song of my well-beloved
Who has me as their God
To protect and provide for them
But forsook me for other gods.

Reflection
Are you faithful to God?
Are you bearing the right fruits?
God wants you to have a harvest.

21

Remembered

For in death there is no remembrance of thee:
In the grave who shall give thee thanks?
(Psalms 6: 5 KJV)

Only remembered by what we have done
Not by the measure of our wealth and riches
Or the vastness of our material possessions
Which we leave behind after we are gone

Only remembered by what we have done
Not by the measure of our talents and gifts
Or the uniqueness of our abilities
Which we fail to use while we are here

Only remembered by what we have done
Not by our lofty dreams and ambitions
Or the greatness of our noble intentions
Which we did nothing about while alive

Only remembered by what we have done
The plans and purposes we accomplished
The lives and things we impacted
With the fleeting time we spent here.

Reflection
*Spend some moments reflecting on what
You will be remembered for.*

22

Die Empty

Whatsoever thy hand findeth to do, do it with thy might;
for there is no work, nor device, nor knowledge,
nor wisdom, in the grave, whither thou goest.
(Ecclesiastes 9: 10 KJV)

We come into the world naked and empty
But for the purpose which occasioned us
And the things needed to accomplish them
We depart the world naked and empty

We come into the world naked and empty
But we labour and strive for more
And are rewarded with abundance
We depart the world naked and empty

We come into the world naked and empty
But we do not know for how long
And our time could come anytime
We depart the world naked and empty

We come into the world naked and empty
But to fulfil a plan and purpose
Which we must endeavour to accomplish
So we can die empty and fulfilled.

Reflection
Is your life driven by God's purpose for you?

23

Six Things God Hates

These six things doth the LORD hate:
Yea, seven are an abomination unto him:
(Proverbs 6: 16 KJV)

Six things the Lord hates
The first is a proud look
Which makes one feel superior
The second is a lying tongue
Which deceives and manipulates

Six things the Lord hates
The third are hands that kill
Which shed the blood of the innocent
The fourth is an evil heart
Which invents wicked plans

Six things the Lord hates
The fifth are mischievous feet
Which run swiftly to evil
The sixth is a false witness
Who breathes out lies

Six things the Lord hates
The seventh is an abomination
A person who sows discord among brethren
These things you must flee from.

Reflection
Have you caught yourself doing any one of these things
that God hates?

24

Beauty Fades

Favour is deceitful, and beauty is vain:
But a woman that feareth the LORD,
she shall be praised.
(Proverbs 31: 30 KJV)

Beauty is desirable
But it fades
Charm is captivating
But it is deceitful
A good character is adorable
It gets better with time

Attraction is strong
But is only for a while
Fashion is classy
But it goes out of style
A kind heart is sweet
It refreshes the soul

Fame is enticing
But it destroys
Richness is reassuring
But is unreliable
Love is better
It overcomes all

Knowledge is power
But it fails
Wisdom is profitable
But is limited
Godliness is the best
It never fails.

Reflection
Are you drawn by godly attributes in other people?
Or are you easily carried away by beauty and fancy?
Beauty fades.

25

Praise God

Praise ye the LORD.
Praise God in his sanctuary:
Praise him in the firmament of his power.
(Psalms 150: 1 KJV)

Praise God
From dawn to dusk
From sunrise to sunset
From this moment to that moment
Let everything praise God

Praise God
From year to year
From season to season
Every moment of every day
Let everything praise God

Praise God
In good times and in bad times
In scarcity and in abundance
Every moment of every day
Let everything praise God

Praise God
In sickness and in health
In life and in death
Every moment of every day
Let everything praise God

Praise God
For all that He is
For all that He has done
For all that He will do
Let everything praise God.

Reflection
Isn't God worthy of every praise?

Devotionals

DEVOTIONALS

26

Godly Nature

And one cried unto another, and said,
Holy, holy, holy, is the LORD of hosts:
(Isaiah 6: 3 KJV)

Holiness sums up the totality of who and what God is. The word "holy" is derived from an old English word *hāl* meaning "whole" and is used to mean uninjured, sound, healthy, entire, complete. Holy therefore denotes perfection and is defined as "exalted or worthy of complete devotion as one perfect in goodness and righteousness." God is simply perfect! There is no impurity, corruption, shortcoming, or weakness with God, instead He is perfect in every way. Perfect is what God is, and if we aspire to be like Him, we should seek perfection.

While we could never be entirely perfect, by possessing all the required or desirable characteristics of God, we could at least strive for perfection by endeavouring to possess as many godly characteristics as we possibly can. We can aspire to be as good as is possible for us to be. Likewise, while we may never be perfect, we can always be better than we previously were or had been.

Pursuing godliness is not necessarily a lofty ambition but it is a necessity for anyone who wishes to be a child of God. Children usually look like their parents and share some physical and behavioural characteristics with them, such that it is possible to easily identify whose child a person is simply by carefully observing such a person's looks and behaviour. In the animal world, the offspring of particular types of animals resemble their parents while in the plant kingdom also, young plants or seedlings resemble their parent plant (if not at the early stages, then as their growth progresses). Therefore, the best way we can demonstrate that we are children of God is to exhibit godly characteristics as much as possible. Some of the divine characters of God are revealed in the "fruits of the spirit" which include love, joy, peace, longsuffering, gentleness, goodness, faith, meekness, and temperance (Galatians 5: 22–23). To be godly therefore is to bear these and other godly fruits.

Reflection
Are you a child of God?
Do you look and act like God in your behaviour?
You can and should.

27

Love

Hatred stirs up strife,
But love covers and overwhelms all transgressions
[forgiving and overlooking another's faults].
(Proverbs 10: 12 AMP)

We all owe our existence to the love of God, thus love is the force that governs all of creation. Love is life and life is love, therefore, to truly love is to truly live. God expects us to love as He loves us. Love is the connection between God and humans and other creatures, between humans and other things created, and between humans. Therefore, living would almost be impossible in the absence of love. But what exactly is love?

The conventional definition of love is flawed in many ways. Love, for instance, is wrongly perceived as a feeling, an emotional attachment or expression. Love, however, is not just a feeling because although it can be felt, it is a tangible state of being, a divine entity or spiritual force which is personified in and through humans. Putting it succinctly, God is love, which means that to love is to reflect an attribute of God's. This also implies that we cannot love unless we allow God to operate in and through us, since we cannot give what we do not have. Even when we have something, it is possible not to share it with others, if we do not want to.

The decision to love, therefore, is a choice we have to make before we can love as we should, unconditionally. It means we do not love people because they are deserving of our love or because we consider them worthy to be loved, but simply because they are God's creation. It is common for us to refuse to love someone who might have hurt us, falsely accused or maligned us, or who is simply mean or wicked in their deeds. Incidentally, we fail to love under such circumstances perhaps mainly because of our flawed understanding of what love is.

We therefore need to understand that true love is unconditional, is not purposed for selfish reasons, is not self-centred, and it is not by individual ability but rather by divine enabling. We also need to understand that to love others is a divine instruction which, actually, is for our benefit on an individual and collective basis. We need to love always and not hate.

Reflection
Do you love others as God requires you to?
If you desire to, with God's help you can.

28

Joy

Therefore with joy shall ye draw water
out of the wells of salvation.
(Isaiah 12: 3 KJV)

Joy is presented as a fruit of the spirit and is defined as a feeling of great pleasure and happiness. Joy is a godly nature that ensures that regardless of what is happening around us, we remain happy. We are supposed to rejoice or be happy at all times; not because everything will be good always but because God is able to and will use everything, good or bad, to bring about our good. Joy at all times regardless of circumstance is also a strong demonstration of faith and hope in God, which are both fruits of the spirit also, and thus also reflect the depth of our intimacy with God.

We can cultivate the character of joy by acquiring a deeper knowledge and understanding of who God is. The more we know God, the more we realise that nothing could ever happen without His knowledge and permission, and also that He is perfect and all his ways are perfect. We would then also realise that God could not ordain or allow anything to happen to or around us except such things are intended for our good. We would also realise that God works in different ways to manifest His intended goodness, such that He sometimes takes us through bad situations but only to bring us to a good end. Consequently, these realisations would make it possible and perhaps easier maintaining an attitude of joy as a permanent personal characteristic.

When our joy or happiness is rooted solely in God, our knowledge of who and what He is as well as our personal relationship with Him, and not on our emotions, circumstances, or material possessions, joy becomes a personal attribute which is not dependent on events or circumstances. It would then become a permanent nature of ours.

Reflection
Is joy part of your nature?
Make God the source of your joy.

29

Peace

Great peace have they which love thy law:
And nothing shall offend them.
(Psalms 119: 165 KJV)

Peace represents freedom from disturbance in any form or size and is a godly nature. It is more a state of being than a feeling or state of mind. Real peace could not exist outside of God because only in God is peace guaranteed and obtainable. Real peace, therefore, can only be found in God whose nature also includes peace. Perhaps it is for this reason that peace seems to have eluded the world today, and has become a scarce but much-coveted commodity, because the world has forsaken God who created us, abandoning His laws and ways.

We, however, should not allow ourselves to conform to the worldly standard where peace is almost an illusion and unattainable but instead we should endeavour to cultivate peace as part of our nature. A peaceful nature ensures that we remain undisturbed regardless of what we encounter in life; be it death, failure, disappointment, famine, sickness, hurt, or any other challenges. When peace is part of our nature, we do not only have peace all the time within and without us, but we also would relate with everyone around us with peace. Only those who have peace or are peace-filled can be peaceful and extend peace to the people around them.

Peace is acquired through intimacy with God including abiding within His   will for us and also observing to do every of His commandment. When we abide in God's will for us, we can rest assured that nothing could by any means harm or disappoint us. Observing the things God has commanded us to do would also ensure that we lived peaceably with everyone else at all times, as well as being peacemakers between other people where we have the opportunity of doing so. Peace as a nature makes us easily recognisable as children of God.

Reflection
Spend some moments reflecting on the peace we have in God.
Pray for a peaceful nature.

30

Longsuffering

Many are the afflictions of the righteous:
But the LORD delivereth him out of them all.
(Psalms 34: 19 KJV)

A rare strength of character is the ability to endure hardship or unpleasant situations over a prolonged period while maintaining the right attitude without becoming easily irritable, angry, or bitter. The ability to endure for long, or longsuffering, is a godly nature. As the strength of a man is revealed not in what he is able to do, but by what he is able to endure, so does longsuffering reveal more of our godly nature than some of the other fruits of the spirit. Longsuffering incorporates endurance and patience and is more than each of these virtues.

The godly nature of longsuffering, therefore, embodies patience which is defined as the ability or capacity to accept or tolerate delay, problems, or suffering without becoming annoyed, embittered, or anxious. Longsuffering also embodies endurance which is defined as the ability to endure, to suffer patiently in an unpleasant or difficult process or situation without giving way (i.e., quitting or surrendering). This godly nature thus enables us not only to endure or handle difficult challenges but to do so with the right attitude, while also not losing hope or giving up.

What can make us be willing and able to suffer for long with a right attitude without giving up? Answer: When we truly realise that God loves us unconditionally, is all-knowing, ever-present, all-powerful, is always in control, and will make everything to work together for our good.

Longsuffering has its benefits. If patience has its reward, then longsuffering has even greater rewards. People like Noah, Abraham, Joseph, Hannah, and Job who patiently endured very unpleasant circumstances over a very long time while persistently trusting and hoping in God, eventually received more than they expected. So shall we when we make longsuffering a part of our godly nature.

Reflection
Are you willing to endure hardship for God's sake?
Our calling requires we do.

31

Gentleness

A soft and gentle and thoughtful answer turns away wrath,
But harsh and painful and careless words stir up anger.
(Proverbs 15: 1 AMP)

To be regarded as a gentleman in the world today is to be seen as
honourable, courteous, or chivalrous, and it is a much-desired
compliment. Although a gentleman and gentleness are closely
related, gentleness is far more than simply being a gentleman.
Gentleness is defined as the quality of being kind, tender or
mild-mannered, which are all types of godly nature.
To be kind, courteous, or mild-mannered in today's world is not
quite popular and is easily mistaken for weakness, based on
conventional standards. Gentleness, however, is a strength and not
a weakness. We should understand that worldly wisdom does not
always agree with godly wisdom, in fact, both are opposed to each
other in most cases. Likewise, those things considered weak by worldly
standards are often the things that are considered mighty by godly

standards. So, while gentleness may be considered outdated and out-of-fashion by the world, it is our responsibility as the children of God to cultivate it so that it becomes a part of our nature. We can do this by refusing to conform to the world, and by abiding in God's grace and will, which would enable and empower us with the nature of gentleness.

Gentleness will make us resemble more of God than the world.

Reflection
Would you rather be praised by the world or commended by God?
God's commendation is better.

32

Goodness

For the Lord is good;
His mercy and lovingkindness are everlasting,
His faithfulness [endures] to all generations.
(Psalms 100: 5 AMP)

God is good always and forever, and everything about Him including his deeds and handwork are good. Goodness is therefore, a godly nature which everyone who aspires to live godly should possess. Goodness is defined as the quality of being morally good or virtuous, and it has the same meaning as righteousness, uprightness, integrity, dignity, respectability, principle, and nobility.

The godly nature of goodness is not to be confused with an individual's ability to do some good from time to time, it is not of self nor is it based on morality or principle, but it is a state of being realisable through intimacy with God such that God's Spirit is alive in us to the extent of being in control of our thoughts and actions. Goodness, as every other nature of God, is not conditional because it is not dependent on circumstances but instead it remains unchanged and undiminished regardless of the situation. In other words, we are not only good to people who are good to us or who deserve to be treated nicely, but to everyone. Likewise, we are not only good when things are good but we remain good no matter the condition.

The same way God's goodness is unchanging and unfailing to everyone, and follows us all the days of our lives, is the same way our goodness should be when goodness becomes part of our godly nature. Goodness would then become a fruit we bear in all seasons.

Reflection
Will you always be good to everyone as God is?

33

Faith

*But without faith it is impossible to [walk with God and]
please Him, for whoever comes [near] to God must
[necessarily] believe that God exists and that He rewards
those who [earnestly and diligently] seek Him.*
(Hebrews 11: 6 AMP)

Before we can possess godly characteristics, we must have a
relationship with God; and before we can relate with God, we must
first know who and what God is. Since God is spirit, a vital
prerequisite for knowing and relating with Him is faith because it
is impossible to see God visibly. Only by faith are we able to
confidently believe in what we have not and cannot see. Hence this
admonition: *"Look at the proud one, His soul is not right within him, But
the righteous will live by his faith [in the true God]* (Habakkuk 2: 4 AMP).

Living, for the righteous, is by faith which is also a godly nature.
Faith in this context relates to faith in God where faith is defined as a
complete trust or confidence in God. We couldn't truly be God's
children if we found it difficult trusting Him. Practically every aspect

of our relationship and interaction with God is hinged on faith in Him. From believing that God exists, loves us unconditionally, intends good for us, is faithful, capable, reliable, dependable, to believing every word of God including his promises, all require faith in God.

Faith is not automatic but is acquired through intimacy with God. Hearing God speak either through written scripture or directly to us engenders faith. Reading about God's great and mighty deeds in the Bible helps us develop faith in God. Witnessing God do things in our lives and in the lives of other people also builds faith in us. Testimony; ours and those of others, is a good faith-builder. Furthermore, constant communication with God through prayers and supplication also helps to solidify our faith. It is worth pointing out that it is our responsibility to cultivate and build our faith in God. We have to be intentional in this regard.

Faith also grows out of usage because, just as practice makes perfect, the more we exercise our faith, the more it grows stronger and bigger. Indeed, one of the most effective ways of developing faith in God is by putting it to test by exercising it. Sometimes, God makes us wait or puts our faith to test in many other ways in order to help it grow.

Faith is a vital necessity which we couldn't live without and so must cultivate.

Reflection
Are you living by faith?

34

Meekness

Meekness is another endangered godly nature in today's world. It is endangered because it is considered outdated and not compatible with modern worldly standards. Meekness, however, is a precious and very rewarding virtue and is defined as the condition of being meek, which is defined as to be quiet, gentle, easily imposed on, and to be submissive. Being easily imposed on or being submissive could easily be regarded as a weakness, shortcoming, or even deficiency, but not when God is the other party in the equation.

Meekness, as a godly nature, relates to our submissiveness to God, making us easily teachable. It is nothing close to being a pushover, gullible or prone to manipulation by other people but instead being submissive to God. This clarification is necessary because being sheepishly submissive to a human being could render us vulnerable to manipulation and abuse. While humans can be deceptive and dishonest, God cannot be any of that, meaning we risk nothing by being submissive to God. On the contrary, submission to God is the most rewarding and the best thing we could do for ourselves.

Meekness implies subjecting human wisdom, including our own, to God's wisdom, relying on God instead of on our abilities, trusting God more than our instincts, bringing our will and desire in conformity with God's will for us, doing things not because we can but only if required of us by God, and doing everything we do not for vain glory but to the glory of God alone.

Reflection
Spend some moments reflecting on meekness as a godly nature.
Ask God to anoint you with the spirit of meekness.

35

Temperance

Like a city that is broken down and without walls
[leaving it unprotected]
Is a man who has no self-control over his spirit
[and sets himself up for trouble].
(Proverbs 25: 28 AMP)

Temperance as a godly nature is defined as moderation or voluntary self-restraint. It is one of the six virtues in the positive psychology classification alongside wisdom, courage, humanity, justice, and transcendence. Another word for temperance is self-control, which is defined as the ability to exercise restraint over ourselves or keep oneself (thought and action) in check when and where necessary.

A person without self-control is an accident waiting to happen or a ticking time bomb. People, for instance, become addicted to alcohol not because of having tasted alcohol but due to failure in controlling how much alcohol they drink, or could be provoked to commit murder not because they were angry but because they failed to control the anger, or they could embezzle public fund not only because they had access to such monies but due to their lack of self-restraint. The lack of self-control is emasculating as it renders victims very susceptible to influences which otherwise are powerless over them but which become very powerful due to a lack of self-restraint.

On the other hand, temperance, is very empowering as it places us firmly in control of the situation and beyond vulnerability to undue influences. Joseph and Daniel are good examples of people who demonstrated self-control when faced with tempting challenges. Joseph overcame lust and adultery and Daniel refused to eat food forbidden by God and was ultimately rewarded as a result. David, Solomon, and Saul, on the other hand, demonstrated their lack of self-control when also faced with tempting challenges; David committed adultery and murder, Solomon fell into idolatry and Saul took things forbidden by God thereby dishonouring God. All these offences had serious consequences.

Temperance helps to preserve and protect us from avoidable danger and is cultivated intentionally as a matter of personal choice.

Reflection
Do you have self-control?

36

Abiding In God

*He that dwelleth in the secret place of the Most High
Shall abide under the shadow of the Almighty.*
(Psalms 91: 1 KJV)

To be like God, we first need to know Him, which requires that we spend reasonable time with Him. We need to dwell in God's presence for us to abide in Him. Dwelling in God's presence involves spending time with God's word in order to uncover God's particular will and plan for us individually and through us for the world we live in. This would include our need to possess godly nature because God desires us to resemble Him in character and behaviour. Therefore, to transform from a fallen, sinful nature into a likeness of God, we need to abide in God continually.

For untrained eyes, fruit-bearing trees are often identified not by the trees themselves but by the fruits they bring forth. While experts in plant studies could easily identify a particular plant from its seed or seedling, many who are without much training in plants rely on other signs, usually the fruits. Be that as it may, some trees sometimes fail to bear fruits for one reason or another. It is possible, for instance, to come across an apple tree barren of fruits during fruiting season. This is usually an indication that something was wrong with the tree. At other times it could be a single branch without fruits, in which case, the problem is usually localised to the particular barren branch, which could be one or another thing including diseases and disconnection. The latter, disconnection, is a common reason for branches to become diseased, barren of fruits, or to whither.

Once properly connected to the parent plant, a branch is supplied with everything needed to stay healthy and fruitful, but once disconnection occurs, due to any reason, a breach in the supply of life-giving nutrients from the parent tree to the branch results in malnutrition and malfunctioning including failure to bear fruits. Likewise, we need to stay permanently connected to God if we are to thrive. God is our life-giver because we became living souls as a result of His breath which effectively is the human spirit. Hence, it is with our spirit that we connect and relate with God. It is with our spirit that we abide in God.

Abiding with and in God requires us to be spirit-minded and spirit-led such that we live and make decisions informed and influenced by our spirit instead of the mind. The godly nature is acquired and expressed from the spirit and not the mind, which in most cases is opposed to godliness. It would be difficult, for instance, to rejoice in the face of adversity from the mind but easier when we engage our spirit because the spirit is not bound by natural circumstances. We, therefore, need to ensure that our spirit permanently abides in God.

Reflection
Are you abiding in God?

37

Hope In God

Why art thou cast down, O my soul? And why art thou disquieted in me?
Hope thou in God: For I shall yet praise him For the help of his countenance.
O my God, my soul is cast down within me: Therefore will I remember thee
from the land of Jordan, and of the Hermonites, from the hill Mizar. Deep
calleth unto deep at the noise of thy waterspouts: All thy waves and thy
billows are gone over me. Yet the LORD will command his lovingkindness in
the daytime, And in the night his song shall be with me, and my prayer unto
the God of my life. I will say unto God my rock, why hast thou forgotten me?
Why go I mourning because of the oppression of the enemy? As with a sword
in my bones, Mine enemies reproach me; While they say daily unto me,
Where is thy God? Why art thou cast down, O my soul? And why art thou
disquieted within me? Hope thou in God; For I shall yet praise him, who is the
health of my countenance, and my God.
(Psalm 42: 5–11 KJV)

Life is like a roller-coaster; sometimes it takes us up, sometimes it
brings us down. When we are up in the high mountains of life, being
happy and thankful comes easily and naturally but not so when life

takes us deep down in its valleys. The mountain and valley seasons of life are common to everyone and are both integral to existence. Interestingly, each season is not without a purpose and benefit. Each season also requires different strategies in order to fully derive the associated benefit. We, for instance, must not allow ourselves to get carried away while at the mountain top and we must also refuse to be overwhelmed by despair or distress when down in the valley.

How can we cope well in the valley? Have you ever found yourself so down or low-spirited that you feel very helpless praying or praising God? Or such that the last thing you want to do is have anything to with God? A situation brought about by perhaps an ongoing challenge, illness, loss of a loved one, heartbreak, business or academic failure, or betrayal by a trusted friend? Oftentimes, a common response when this happens is to be withdrawn into self-isolation which could culminate in a pity party, with the result that we may even become depressed eventually. David, the Psalmist, found himself in one of such down moments but he handled it very well. What did David do when his soul was cast down?

He kept his hope in God alive. How did he do this? He spoke to himself: "Soul, hope thou in God, do not give up just now please. Hang in there because I will yet praise Jehovah! It may seem like it is all over for me now but I know Jehovah will not abandon me. He will see me through. My Soul, be strong and stay with me." David made himself strong in the Lord, he refused to cave in and allow his feelings rule him. He fought with despair, depression, anguish, anxiety, fear, name it, but he did not lose hope. And then David also spoke with God, even though he was downcast.

Like David, when we find ourselves in the valley, it is time for us to bring to bear everything we have learnt in our walk with God in encouraging ourselves. The valley season is not a time to let go of our faith and hope in God or to easily forget our testimony of how God has brought us this far. It is a season when we call God's faithfulness in our lives to remembrance, when we refuse to be overwhelmed but instead, keep up keeping up. It is the time when we intentionally encourage ourselves. Very much like advice, the best encouragement is the one we give ourselves. We must speak up our hope till it rises, and pray and praise till strength rises from within. Like David also, we should talk to God, not by accusing Him of abandoning or forgetting us but by reminding Him of the many things He has done for us in the past, as David did.

It is worth pointing out that our faith and relationship with God is not based on feelings. Therefore, we must not allow our feelings determine how we relate with God or our faith in Him. "Though He slays me yet will I trust in Him" should be our motto. Feelings come and feelings go but God's love and steadfastness remain forever. While in the valley, we must endeavour to keep our hope in God alive and strong because this is the right response to the valley season.

Reflection
Are you down in the valley now?
Remember that the God of the mountains
is still the God in the valley.
Hope in God.

38

The Great Deliverer

Many hardships and perplexing circumstances confront the righteous, But the Lord rescues him from them all.
(Psalm 34:19 AMP)

Who in this world is without a challenge? Who has never encountered perplexing circumstances in life? Who has never experienced hardship in life? Perhaps, nobody. Hard times, difficult challenges, and vicissitudes are common to all people regardless of status or background. Therefore, we are not to become perplexed when we encounter affliction in life. We should instead acknowledge affliction as integral to our existence here. As the saying goes, to be forewarned is to be forearmed, therefore, hardship should not take us by surprise even if they come upon us unexpectedly. Also, our understanding that we would encounter difficult situations in life should equip us with the ability and preparedness to effectively handle them whenever we eventually encounter hardship in life.

Fortunately, we have the promise of deliverance by God from every hardship or affliction that we could ever encounter in life. How refreshing! In Psalms 46: 1 we read: *God is our refuge and strength [mighty and impenetrable], A very present and well-proved help in trouble* (AMP). Are we not glad that we have God to run to when troubles come? It is up to us, however, to run to God for deliverance in times of trouble. Problem arises when instead of God, we run to other alternatives which offer no real solution to the challenging situation but instead, empty promises and false assurances. When, for instance, we simply run to particular people for assistance, perhaps because we think they are capable of helping us in particular situations, instead of allowing God direct us to those He appointed to assist us, we risk facing disappointment in addition to leaving the problem unresolved. Likewise, when we put all our trust in experts, such as medical, financial, business, or relationship experts, instead of God's guidance and direction, we are unlikely to experience the deliverance promised by God.

We must come to the point where we thoroughly understand that only God is able to deliver us from every situation and that God is the primary and ultimate provider for everyone regardless of the way and means God chooses to make such provision available to us. When we do, it becomes easy for us to always run to God first for deliverance when trouble comes. And God always delivers!

Reflection
Are you afflicted?
Deliverance belongs to God.
Run to God.

39

The Great Provider

It is vain for you to rise early, To retire late,
To eat the bread of anxious labors— For He gives [blessings]
to His beloved even in his sleep.
(Psalm 127: 2 AMP)

God the life-giver is also the provider for everything needed to
sustain, prosper, and accomplish each life. God is the primary and
ultimate provider for all creation, being responsible for existence in
the first place. It would not seem right that God should create us and
then leave it to us to provide for ourselves such things as needed to
sustain life and thrive. Going by convention, however, the following
are revealed with respect to our daily needs and provision: First, we
behave as though our provisions depend solely on our own efforts.
Second, we seem to forget that "bread through sweat" is actually a
curse associated with disobedience to God (see Genesis 3: 17–19). We
behave as though we believe that we are solely responsible for our
provisions.

Although we each have roles to play in the realisation of our daily provision, it is necessary that we properly understand that every provision comes from God, whose original intention was not for us to sweat excessively before we can eat bread. Excessive labour is actually a consequence of our fallen nature and is often used by the enemy of mankind to distract us from the more important things we are meant to do here, by ensuring that we spend most of our time preoccupied with "making a living." Ironically, and very sadly, many people in trying to make a living fail to actually live, having invested the time they should have used to truly live in ceaseless labour. Which somehow begs this question: *What profit hath a man of all his labour which he taketh under the sun?* (Ecclesiastes 1: 3 KJV). Do you know?

These testimonies further attest to God's faithfulness in providing for us: *I have been young, and now am old; Yet have I not seen the righteous forsaken, nor his seed begging bread. He is ever merciful, and lendeth; And his seed is blessed* (Psalm 37: 25–26 KJV). And, *Can a woman forget her sucking child, that she should not have compassion on the son of her womb? yea, they may forget, yet will I not forget thee. Behold, I have graven thee upon the palms of my hands; thy walls are continually before me* (Isaiah 49: 15–16 KJV). We stand to gain a lot when we realise that God is our provider and thus trust Him for guidance to the means for each provision.

Reflection
Do you recognise God as your provider?

40

Train Up A Child

Train up a child in the way he should go
[teaching him to seek God's wisdom and
will for his abilities and talents],
Even when he is old he will not depart from it.
(Proverbs 22: 6 AMP)

Parental responsibility is a divinely-ordained duty of every parent (not just biological parents but every adult responsible for any young person) and also a natural right. While we focus on building up ourselves, spiritually and otherwise, it is also necessary that we endeavour to develop ourselves in parenting. The need to bring up our children and other young people in our care cannot be overemphasised. It is a matter of making or destroying lives. We are largely products of the type of parenting and upbringing we were exposed to from childhood. With the benefit of matured insight and hindsight, we can look back through time and decide what and where our parents got it right with us and where they did not.

Consequently, we should be better informed about what parenting skills and practices we can adopt from our parents and those we should either discard or improve upon.

Parenting is a great responsibility that we must never neglect, delegate, or abdicate. God expects every parent to be hands-on in the upbringing of the children He has given them because God has specifically equipped each set of parents with everything needed for the right upbringing of the particular children brought into life through them, including patience. The upbringing we expose our children to reflects the kind of adults we desire them to become because the training children receive determines how they turn out as adults. Therefore, if we desire our children to become responsible adults, for instance, we must then train them in being responsible from childhood.

With respect to training up a child, it is important that we realise that with children there is more caught than is taught. This simply means that children learn more from the behaviour they observe from their parents and those around them than the habits they are theoretically taught; thus implying that the best training we can give to our children is being practical role models through our conduct. We, for instance, have to exemplify godly nature through our daily actions if we desire for our children to grow up into godly people. It is not enough to teach them things contained in the word of God without living by those examples. Regardless of what we say to them, it is what we do that our children will do.

Due to modern trends, including governmental policies in parts of the world which tend to control parental disciplining, we must realise that it is our primary responsibility to bring up our children in a right and reasonable manner, as instructed by God. We are accountable to God in this regard and not to any other authority. We must also realise that our children cannot overpower us when it comes to raising them up rightly, either due to stubbornness or unruliness, or else God would not have committed them into our care for their upbringing. With God's help, if we are determined to bring up our children God's way, we can   overcome every challenge and train up our children in the way they should go.

Reflection
Are you a positive role model to the children in your care?
God expects and requires you to.

41

Let God Arise

Let God arise, let his enemies be scattered:
Let them also that hate him flee before him.
As smoke is driven away, so drive them away:
As wax melteth before the fire,
so let the wicked perish at the presence of God.
But let the righteous be glad; let them rejoice before God:
Yea, let them exceedingly rejoice.
(Psalm 68:1–3 KJV)

As we go through life, we are bound to encounter opposition in
one way or another. Some oppositions could be stiff enough to
pressure us into giving up on a pursuit or even on life itself, while
others could even be life-threatening such that our lives could be at
risk. Opposition, however, should not be strange to us because it is
almost a natural aspect of life here on earth. Fortunately, no
opposition could arise without God allowing it. And we know that
God's ultimate plan for everyone is for good. We, however, need to do

something when opposition arises if we are to realise God's good plans for us.

What should we do when faced with opposition? Analyse and talk about it? Indulge in the blame game or self-pity? Surrender and retreat? Or bemoan our fate? None of the mentioned is productive and none would help us face and overcome the opposition in order to eventually realise God's hidden goodness in the situation. What we need to do is to call unto God!

God instructs us as follows: *And call upon me in the day of trouble: I will deliver thee, and thou shalt glorify me* (Psalm 50:15 KJV). God desires to deliver us from every opposition and trouble hence this instruction. God also promises to deliver us when we do. And God will!

Whenever opposition arises against us, our first response should be to call to God to arise. Jehovah is a Man of War and is mighty in battle; when He arises, every opposition and enemies are scattered. We should also call God to arise on behalf of other people we know when they face opposition, perhaps family members, friends, neighbours, colleagues or even strangers. We are supposed to be our "brother's keeper", so we should lend a helping hand in any way we can to anyone we see who is challenged or in trouble. This is more honourable and rewarding than merely discussing our problems or those of others with people.

We could even call such people and pray with them if we have the opportunity. Or we could even organise a quick intercession with family or friends to pray for those we know who are facing challenges. Imagine what would happen if we all did this instead of looking after only ourselves and our own or simply talking about the problem. It would be a different and better world.

Reflection
*How would you respond when
faced with opposition or trouble?*

42

Broken And Crushed

The LORD is nigh unto them that are of a broken heart;
And saveth such as be of a contrite spirit.
(Psalms 34: 18 KJV)

Certain experiences or circumstances in life leave our hearts broken and our spirits crushed. The death of a loved one or family member, for instance, could bring us so much grief and anguish, leaving us disconsolate. A failed relationship or marriage could also fill us with despair and take a huge toll on our confidence. Disappointment from close and trusted friends or family members could also leave us broken, forlorn, and unable to trust again. These and other circumstances often fill us with grief. Coping with grief is not very easy, and when not handled very well, grieving could affect our health adversely.

Comfort is the antidote for grief because it gradually but effectively releases our hearts from grief, thus counteracting the unpleasant feeling we get while grieving. God is the only reliable source of comfort and is always very near to those who grief or are broken-hearted. When we make an effort to avail ourselves of the comfort God makes available to us when we look to Him in times of grief and brokenness, we will experience such freedom from pain and grief as we never imagined is possible. God's comfort reaches the root of the grief, where the healing begins, thus ensuring that the grief we feel is completely uprooted and not just partly trimmed.

Death is one of the many causes of grief that is hard to comprehend or handle, perhaps because death represents a finality. When we lose a loved one to death, there is no chance of that person returning to life, and that alone is much pain. However, God's comfort in this regard helps us to realise that the life of the departed was a gift to us from God. Since God gave, then it is also up to Him to take. This realisation should then engender gratitude in us towards God for blessing us with the life of the departed person. A change in attitude, which in turn would ameliorate our grief subsequently eliminating it completely. This is an example of how God deals with our grief from its roots.

When we allow God, He is able to comfort us regardless of the circumstance thus bringing healing to our brokenness and wholeness to our wounds.

Reflection
Are you broken or crushed?
Suffering from grief?
God is willing and able to comfort you.

43

The Gift Of Life

Let the day perish wherein I was born,
And the night in which it was said,
There is a man child conceived.
(Job 3: 3 KJV)

There are times in life when we may wish we were never born, perhaps due to one nagging problem or another. This was the case with Job after he lost all his children and wealth in a single day, followed by physical ailment and false accusations from close friends. We may never experience a fraction of what Job went through, but many other situations could make us wish we were never born. A person who was abandoned at birth by both parents could sometimes wish as Job did, due to the pain associated with such abandonment. A person who was betrayed by a marital partner after several years of marriage, leading to a separation or divorce, may also wish they were never born. There are many other circumstances that could make us despise our lives.

We must, however, never despise our lives because to each of us, it is a gift from God. None of us asked to be born nor played any role in our birth. God is fully responsible for our existence, having decided to form us in our mother's womb, and for a reason. Consequently, no matter the particular circumstances associated with our birth or that we may encounter in the course of living, may we always acknowledge that our life is a gift from God not only to ourselves but to the world. Furthermore, we must also remember that whatever God allows us to experience is done for a reason and always for our good. And also that God is able to use every situation, no matter how sad or bad, to accomplish His good plans for us. These are enough to make us value and appreciate our lives as well as circumstances instead of despising our existence or bemoaning our fate.

Whatever our parents, spouses, friends, or anyone else have done to us, we must realise that God and not them gave us life and is the reason we are alive. Therefore, we should not allow how others treat us make us despise our lives thus becoming ungrateful to God for our existence. We should always recognise God as the only reason we exist and look to Him in every circumstance. When we do, we are bound to appreciate the gift that is the life we are given which in turn would make us always grateful. Gratitude will ensure that we get the best out of life including from such circumstances that ordinarily would make us wish we were never born.

Reflection
Are you grateful for your life?

44

~~~~~~~~~~

A Little Oil

But she said, "As the Lord your God lives, I have no bread,
only a handful of flour in the bowl and a little oil in the jar.
See, I am gathering a few sticks so that I may go in and bake it
for me and my son, that we may eat it [as our last meal] and die."
(1 Kings 17: 12 AMP)

A little goes a long way when God is involved because God who is
able to create something out of nothing is also able to stretch
something little beyond its ordinary capacity. When Elijah the
prophet requested a meal from the widow of Zarephath, she only had
barely enough for the last meal for herself and her only son. She only
had a handful of flour in a bowl and a little oil in a jar. Yet when
persuaded by the prophet she went ahead to prepare a meal for Elijah
first as he had requested. A miracle happened! *She went and did as*
Elijah said. And she and he and her household ate for many days. The bowl of
flour was not exhausted nor did the jar of oil become empty, in accordance

with the word of the Lord which He spoke through Elijah (1 Kings 17: 15–16 AMP).

The secret behind this miracle can be found in the last phrase of verse sixteen. It happened as God had spoken to Elijah. God's word never fails! However, for the miracle to happen, Elijah had to believe God and act based on his faith. And so, he persuaded the widow to go ahead and grant him his request while reassuring her, in the fourteenth verse, with what God had told him earlier. Having completed his part, it was now the widow's turn to have faith in God's word and exercise such faith. She did! Even though she did not hear from God directly.

The result was that God's word was fulfilled.

We are also sometimes faced with situations where we have little or nothing to accomplish what needs to be done. However, when God tells us what to do about the situation, it is our responsibility to trust Him and to do exactly as instructed. When we do, we are bound to also experience the miracle of accomplishing a great lot with very little.

Reflection
Do you trust God can do a lot
with the very little you have?

45

Manna From Heaven

He lay down and slept under the juniper tree, and behold,
an angel touched him and said to him, "Get up and eat."
He looked, and by his head there was a bread cake baked on hot coal,
and a pitcher of water. So he ate and drank and lay down again.
(1 Kings 19: 5–6 AMP)

There is a common saying in some quarters to the effect that "manna will not fall from heaven," implying that we should not expect God to do things for us, which He has given us the ability to do for ourselves. This is partly true but not always the case. The analogy of mana not falling from heaven is an anomaly because the only mana we know of fell from heaven when God fed the Israelites as they travelled through the wilderness. So, mana actually did fall from heaven! A different form of mana also fell from heaven for Elijah, who at the time had given up on life, wishing to die instead, when an angel woke him up to eat food which Elijah had no hand in preparing.

While there is some truth in the idea that God will not do for us the things He has already empowered us to do and so are supposed to do for ourselves, we should be careful not to underestimate God's ability and willingness to go contrary to convention in order to help us accomplish the things He has ordained for us to do. There are times when we find ourselves in a humanly impossible situation having stepped out in faith to obey God's direction and guidance. Like when the Israelites embarked on a journey from Egypt to the region of Canaan, a journey that eventually lasted about forty years. While in transit, it is very difficult, if not outright impossible, planting and growing your own food. Consequently, when the food they left Egypt with got exhausted, naturally, God took it upon himself to provide for them and thus rained down mana from heaven so they do not starve. God also provided them with meat in the form of quails, and water from the rock because the wilderness they travelled through was a desert. In the case of Elijah also, God provided food for him during a famine using a raven and, on a different occasion, Elijah was presented with a readymade meal having been woken up by an angel. Note how God did not instruct Elijah through the angel to get up and find something to eat. Instead, God provided him with a meal.

When our belief is shaped by some seemingly logical mindsets such that we live by certain human conventions, we risk not experiencing the fullness of what God can do and desires to do in our lives. God's ways are not our ways, and God is not bound by human convention but will do whatever He feels necessary in order to accomplish His plan and purpose in our lives and world. We must therefore ensure that we believe only what God says and not human logic. We should place no limits on God.

Reflection
What can God not do for you
when you trust and obey Him?

46

Blessing In Disguise

So he set out and went to Zarephath,
and when he came to the gate of the city, behold,
a widow was there gathering sticks [for firewood].
He called out to her and said,
"Please bring me a little water in a jar, so that I may drink."
As she was going to get it, he called to her and said,
"Please bring me a piece of bread in your hand."
(1 Kings 17: 10–11 AMP)

We know that God has a habit of working in contradictory ways in order to accomplish a plan. Like when at the beginning of creation He called forth light out of darkness. Thus God uses foolishness to confound wisdom and weakness to humble power and might. Similarly, God often sends us blessings packaged as a burden and major breakthroughs hidden in tough challenges. When God sent Elijah to the widow at Zarephath, ostensibly so that she would provide food for Elijah during a time of famine, God had a different plan.

When Elijah eventually got to Zarephath and met with the widow in question, it turned out that she had barely enough to sustain herself and her son till the next day. Imagine the irony! A woman who herself needed food was chosen as a provider for another's need for food. With God, however, nothing is impossible. When Elijah and the widow believed and acted upon the word spoken to Elijah by God, God provided for them till the famine ended. So, in a way, it could be said that it was Elijah who actually provided for the widow and her household, and not the other way round because the divine provision for food came through the prophet who brought the word of God for provision to the widow.

God most likely planned to provide for the widow and her household during the famine; hence, He sent Elijah. Otherwise, God could have continued to provide for Elijah as He did previously using a raven while providing him water in another miraculous way after the brook dried up as a result of the draught. The fact that Elijah arrived just as she was about preparing her last meal adds further weight to this assumption. Imagine what would have become the fate of the widow and her household had she, out of self-preservation, refused to oblige Elijah's request. Her provision was presented in the form of a burden which required her to part with the little she had. Fortunately, she put herself last and God's word first and thus unwittingly availed herself of the intended blessing God had planned for her.

Oftentimes God may place people on our way for us to assist them in one way or another but only so that through our kindness greater doors of provision and opportunity are opened to us.

Reflection
Spend some moments reflecting on how some of your seeming burdens could actually be disguised blessings.

47

Giant-Slayer

So David triumphed over the Philistine with a sling and a stone,
and he struck down the Philistine and killed him;
but there was no sword in David's hand.
(1 Samuel 17: 50 AMP)

David is commonly known as the young boy who defeated and killed a giant, Goliath. It is also common knowledge that David accomplished this feat merely using a sling or catapult and five stones, although Goliath went down on the first shot. While his opponent, Goliath of Gath, was a well-trained soldier and a champion, David was just a shepherd boy who had no military training, which all make David's accomplishments both very unique and highly outstanding. What perhaps is not equally common knowledge would be David's secret weapon with which his feat was accomplished.

When David took up Goliath's challenge against the army of Israel, he did not do so driven by vain ambition, fame, fortune, or the "I can" attitude. He did so in order to redeem the honour and dignity of God's people. Goliath had every morning and evening openly ridiculed and defied Israel's army (and thus the God of Israel also) for forty days.

A chance encounter brought David face-to-face with Goliath's taunting, which vexed the former making him ask as follows: *Then David spoke to the men who were standing by him, "What will be done for the man who kills this Philistine and removes the disgrace [of his taunting] from Israel? For who is this uncircumcised Philistine that he has taunted and defied the armies of the living God?"* (1 Samuel 17: 26 AMP). David came against Goliath for God's glory and not his .

When eventually the battle was set in array between the two men, even before the first shot was fired, a war of words first ensued between the two men. Goliath railed against David while cursing him by his gods. David on the other hand also railed against Goliath while also declaring thus: *Then David said to the Philistine, "You come to me with a sword, a spear, and a javelin, but I come to you in the name of the Lord of hosts, the God of the armies of Israel, whom you have taunted* (1 Samuel 17: 45 AMP). David's confidence and hope for victory rested not in his ability or weapon of choice but the name of his God.

The foregoing, for God's glory and the name of God, both represent David's secret weapon which enabled him to accomplish the great feat of bringing down a giant feared by the whole army of Israel, thus earning him the epithet "giant-slayer." With our faith in God alone, we can accomplish the impossible.

Reflection
What is your confidence and faith founded on?
God or something else?

48

Speed Of Elijah

In a little while the sky grew dark with clouds and wind,
and there were heavy showers. And Ahab mounted
and rode [his chariot] and went [inland] to Jezreel.
Then the hand of the Lord came upon Elijah
[giving him supernatural strength]. He girded up
his loins and outran Ahab to the entrance of Jezreel
[nearly twenty miles].
(1 Kings 18: 45–46 AMP)

Humans are naturally limited in several ways, including in ability and capability. There are certain things we simply cannot do, for instance, fly unaided, remain suspended in the air unassisted, or run at a certain speed. However, God is able to remove these natural limitations and can turn natural to supernatural and ordinary to extraordinary when it becomes necessary to do so. This was the case when God supernaturally empowered Elijah to run faster than a chariot of horses!

Although it is not in God's character to show off what He can do either directly or through humans, when situations call for a demonstration of His power beyond what is natural and ordinary, He will do so. He did so through David defeating Goliath, Moses delivering Israel from Egyptian captivity, Joshua in the fall of Jericho, and Gideon defeating the Midianite army. However, for God to demonstrate these supernatural and extraordinary abilities through us, we must be willing to trust Him to be able to do all things and anything through us, and for His glory alone. This may require us being stripped of things we have become reliant on, which in turn could constitute limitations in a way so that in their absence, we have no other option but to trust solely in God. Such things as our talents and skills, riches and wealth, people we know and are connected with, or even those things we consider possible and impossible. Needless to point out that such stripping is often uncomfortable, gruesome, or very challenging; the good thing is that the ultimate benefit far outweighs every pain.

In our walk with God, we need to ensure that we do not put any limits on Him, and in what He can or cannot do for us or through us, but we must build up our trust in God to the extent that we believe in the supernatural and extraordinary as possibilities in our lives. Through God we can run faster than the fastest horses, run through the enemy troop unscathed, move mountains, bring down fortified walls of restrictions, part impassable seas, roll back time, make the sun to stand still, or do anything else necessary for us to accomplish the things God has planned for us to do in life. We only need to believe.

Reflection
*Do you believe you can operate
in the supernatural through God?*

49

The Fall Of Jericho

So the people shouted [the battle cry],
and the priests blew the trumpets.
When the people heard the sound of the trumpet,
they raised a great shout and the wall [of Jericho] fell down,
so that the sons of Israel went up into the city,
every man straight ahead [climbing over the rubble],
and they overthrew the city.
(Joshua 6: 20 AMP)

The fall of the walls and city of Jericho is a good demonstration of the supernatural possibilities inherent in trusting and obeying God's instructions to the letter. The city itself was heavily fortified with impregnable walls which were so wide that houses were built on them. The city gates were also firmly locked and secured for fear of the Israelites. As such, it was practically impossible for the Israelites to enter the city, especially considering the limited resources available to them in the form of military strength and equipment.

The situation was such that, except for divine intervention, it was impossible for Jericho to fall into the hands of the Israelites. The Israelites, however, had arrived where they were at the time only through God's leading and in accordance with His plan for Israel. God would not bring them this far only to abandon them. God had a plan for the destruction of Jericho, but it was a plan that would be considered ludicrous.

To overcome Jericho, God instructed the Israelites accordingly: *The Lord said to Joshua, "See, I have given Jericho into your hand, with its king and the mighty warriors. Now you shall march around the city, all the men of war circling the city once. You shall do this [once each day] for six days. Also, seven priests shall carry seven trumpets [made] of rams' horns ahead of the ark; then on the seventh day you shall march around the city seven times, and the priests shall blow the trumpets. When they make a long blast with the ram's horn, and when you hear the sound of the trumpet, all the people shall cry out with a great shout (battle cry); and the wall of the city will fall down in its place, and the people shall go up, each man [going] straight ahead [climbing over the rubble]." (Joshua 6: 2–5 AMP)*. How's that for a battle plan!

As laughable as this plan seems, the people of Jericho could probably have been laughing out loud as the Israelites marched around the city walls in obedience to God. When on the seventh day the people shouted having obeyed entirely every of God's instruction, the walls fell. The walls fell without any contact or pressure from the Israelites. Nothing is impossible with God!

The fall of Jericho is a great encouragement for us to trust and obey God as we journey through life, encountering seemingly insurmountable challenges, whatever they may be. When we obey God's directives, regardless of how ludicrous or unrealistic they may seem, we are bound to witness supernatural possibilities in those things and areas which naturally are truly impossible.

Reflection
Would you trust God even if what He instructs you to do makes no sense?

50

Gideon Army

And the Lord told Gideon,
"With the three hundred men who lapped I will rescue you,
and will hand over the Midianites to you.
Let all the other people go, each man to his home."
(Judges 7: 7 AMP)

It is impossible to imagine how a group of three hundred untrained soldiers could defeat a well-trained and well-equipped army, which greatly outnumbered them and possessed military firepower more advanced and superior than their weapons. Or even how anyone would dare to go on such a mission, as these men did. Well, Gideon and his army did, but not driven by selfish ambition, instead, in obedience to God.

The Israelites went contrary to God's commandments, and as a result, God allowed them to be conquered and dominated by the Midianites for seven years. Consequently, Israel was greatly impoverished, and as a result, they cried out to God for deliverance.

In response, God first alerted them about their transgression which led to their captivity before revealing His calling upon Gideon through an angelic visitation. God had a plan for their deliverance, but it was a very unusual one. First, the person chosen to lead the fightback, Gideon, was but a young man who was not even a regular soldier. Then God trimmed down the number of volunteers who had initially answered Gideon's clarion call from thirty-two thousand men to ten thousand and finally to three hundred men. Finally, for the battle itself, no weapon was to be used; instead, God instructed that they went only with trumpets, empty pitchers, and torches. How's that for a battle plan!

This battle plan, nonetheless, resulted in a grand victory after Gideon complied with every instruction: *When three companies blew the trumpets and broke the pitchers, they held the torches in their left hands, and the trumpets in their right hands to blow, and they shouted, "A sword for the Lord and for Gideon!" Then each stood in his place around the camp; and the entire [Midianite] army ran, crying out as they fled. When Gideon's men blew the three hundred trumpets, the Lord set the sword of one [Midianite] against another even throughout the whole army; and the army fled as far as Beth-shittah toward Zererah, as far as the border of Abel-meholah, by Tabbath* (Judges 7: 20–22 AMP). What a victory!

It is worth pointing out that the first instruction God gave to Gideon was to destroy Baal's altar and raise a fresh altar for God where he offered a sacrifice. Baal worship was the root cause of Israel's Midianite conquest and captivity. Having restored this breach, all that was required of Gideon was to trust and obey God for Israel's deliverance.

When we find ourselves in a captive situation, such that we become dominated, oppressed, suppressed, stagnated, or impoverished, may we realise that God alone is able to turn the situation around and already has a plan of deliverance. When we cry to God, as Israel did on this occasion, and we trust and obey everything He instructs us to do, we would experience supernatural victory also.

Reflection
God has a way out of every tight spot.
You only need to partner with Him.
Would you trust and obey God?

51

Hannah's Prayer

Hannah was greatly distressed, and she
prayed to the Lord and wept in anguish.
She made a vow, saying, "O Lord of hosts,
if You will indeed look on the affliction (suffering)
of Your maidservant and remember, and not forget
Your maidservant, but will give Your maidservant a son,
then I will give him to the Lord all the days of his life;
a razor shall never touch his head."
(1 Samuel 1: 10–11 AMP)

Hannah was married to Elkanah, an Ephraimite, who also had another wife called Penninah. While the other wife had children, Hannah had none. Elkanah's special love for Hannah despite her barrenness provoked Penninah to jealousy which caused her to taunt and provoke Hannah bitterly in order to irritate and ridicule her. Naturally, most women having been married would greatly desire to have their own children, which was the case with Hannah.

Interestingly, despite the intense provocation she faced, Hannah did not react or respond to her adversary. Instead, she cried to God.

Every year, Elkanah's family went up to Shiloh for the annual festival during which Hannah would have fervently prayed to God to bless her with at least a child. And each year, Hannah went back home the same way she came, to continue facing humiliation and provocation because she still had no child. On a particular visit to Shiloh, however, Hannah did something different. She prayed a different kind of prayer; she made a vow. She specifically asked for a son whom she promised to dedicate to God's service all the days of his life. It is possible that after several years of consecration and seeking God's face, Hannah's desires became aligned with God's plans for her. Hence she wanted a child not just to satisfy her personal longing but a child that would be used for God's purpose. This made the difference! Hannah went home happy although she was yet to have a child but she knew her request had been granted, especially after the priest also interceded on her behalf.

When faced with challenges that subject us to ridicule and provocation, it is important that we keep our sights on God alone and not to allow ourselves to become distracted by whatever else could be going on around us. Had Hannah shifted her focus from God to react to Penninah, she might not have prevailed. As we keep our sights on God, we also need to get more intimate with Him including seeking out His will and plan for us about the particular challenge and also our lives in general. Oftentimes God unveils his vision for us during times of intense trial. When we align our desires and request to God's will for us, a breakthrough would not only be inevitable but also imminent.

Reflection
*Will you let go of your desires and
surrender to God's will for you instead?*

52

Laban's Conspiracy

Jacob noticed [a change in] the attitude of Laban,
and saw that it was not friendly toward him as before.
(Genesis 31: 2 AMP)

Jacob had run to his uncle, Laban, in Haran for refuge following Esau's plot to kill him after he deceived and robbed the latter of the blessings of his birth-right. The plan was for Jacob to return home in the region of Canaan after Esau's anger and thirst for blood was abated. Jacob would himself be a victim of deception in the hands of his uncle, Laban. After seven years of servitude, he was given the wrong sister as a wife and had to serve an additional seven years for Rachael, the woman he initially desired to marry. Although God greatly prospered Laban through Jacob's service, he was not straightforward with his nephew whom he intended to cunningly retain in perpetual servitude to continue enjoying God's blessings to him through Jacob.

When Jacob requested Laban to set him free to return home, his uncle persuaded him to remain in his service with an offer for any wages Jacob would ask. Both men had a deal, but even then, Laban was treacherous and hatched a plan intended to prevent Jacob from having a fair wage. Nonetheless, Jacob was given a plan by God in a dream that ensured that the flocks gave birth to streaked, spotted, and speckled offspring that would belong to him based on their agreement. With his evil plan thwarted, Laban's attitude towards Jacob changed.

Based on God's instruction to return to the land of his fathers, Jacob secretly removed his family and belongings. He fled Haran without informing Laban, who, went in his pursuit immediately upon discovering what he had done. While on his way, God appeared to Laban in a dream and warned him: *God came to Laban the Aramean in a dream at night and said to him, "Be careful that you do not speak to Jacob, either good or bad"* (Genesis 31: 24 AMP). Laban wanted to keep Jacob a perpetual servant, with no consideration for the latter's future, simply out of selfish interest. But God had a plan for and through Jacob, and so He intervened.

Amazing! God fights for us even when we are unaware that battles are being planned or waged against us, especially when such battles are intended to obstruct God's plans for us. It is very reassuring that God watches over us to ensure that all   of His plans for us would come to fruition and that He will fight off every opposition, obstacle, or distraction on our path, including those we are not even aware of. All we need to do is stay close to God enough to hear what He is telling us at every given time, and having heard from God to do exactly as told.

Reflection
*What secret battles against you that you are
not aware of could God be fighting for you?*

53

Noah's Ark

God said to Noah, "I intend to make an end of all that lives,
for through men the land is filled with violence;
and behold, I am about to destroy them together with the land.
Make yourself an ark of gopher wood; make in it rooms
(stalls, pens, coops, nests, cages, compartments)
and coat it inside and out with pitch (bitumen).
(Genesis 6: 13–14 AMP)

At a time when the entire world revelled in wickedness, and everyone had evil intentions continually, one man found grace in the eyes of God. That man was Noah, whom God instructed to build an ark after deciding to destroy the world due to its sinfulness. Noah's story and the ark is popular, and many people know that Noah obeyed God in building the ark with which his household and the animal kingdom were saved during the flood.

What might not be equally common knowledge is what it really took for Noah to build the ark. First was Noah's faith in God.

When God told Noah that He was going to destroy the world with a flood, the idea of a flood was a strange phenomenon because it had neither rained on the earth nor had the world ever experienced a flood as yet. Noah, therefore, had to believe in something that did not exist as yet but only because God said so. Next, building the ark would have disrupted Noah's normal life. Noah's regular occupation would have suffered as he invested time in the new project. Noah might even have had to divert funds meant for his upkeep towards this project. He also would have had to hire labour, since it is inconceivable that Noah and his three sons alone could build a boat or ship of such magnitude, which meant more expenditure. Furthermore, since he was building something unknown to the people around him (Noah's ark was the first of its kind) and for a seemingly ludicrous reason (the world had not yet experienced rain or flooding at this time and the idea of God destroying the world was simply laughable), Noah would have been subjected to mocking and ridicule. It is possible that some of the people who knew him and what he was doing could have doubted his mental state. Nonetheless, Noah was undeterred but obeyed God.

What do you think would have been Noah's fate and that of his household had he relented in building the ark as instructed due to one reason or another? He would have perished with the rest of the world!

We may never know the full importance of that seemingly little thing God has told us to do. We may even be tempted to resist God when His plans seem contrary to our aspirations or when pursuing such plans turn our lives upside down. We may become discouraged when what God asks us to do is unpopular and could attract us ridicule or embarrassment. We may be tempted to doubt when what God asks us to do is the first of its kind. But we do not know what it will cost to us if we fail to obey God.

Reflection
*Imagine you found yourself in Noah's
shoes today, would you be faithful to God
in doing what He requires you to do?*

54

Jehoshaphat's Victory

When he had consulted with the people,
he appointed those who sang to the Lord and those
who praised Him in their holy (priestly) attire,
as they went out before the army and said,
"Praise and give thanks to the Lord,
for His mercy and lovingkindness endure forever."
When they began singing and praising,
the Lord set ambushes against the sons of Ammon, Moab,
and Mount Seir, who had come against Judah;
so they were struck down [in defeat].
(2 Chronicles 20: 21–22 AMP)

Every war requires the right strategy; there is no one strategy that fits every battle. Jehovah is a Man of War and is mighty in battle. God's battle plans never fail because He is the God of all battles. As the battle plan God gave Judah during the reign of King Jehoshaphat when the Moabites, Ammonites, and Meunites came to war against them.

When King Jehoshaphat heard about the war, he was naturally afraid, but did the right thing: *Then Jehoshaphat was afraid and set himself [determinedly, as his vital need] to seek the Lord; and he proclaimed a fast throughout all Judah. So [the people of] Judah gathered together to seek help from the Lord; indeed they came from all the cities of Judah to seek the Lord [longing for Him with all their heart]* (2 Chronicles 20: 3–4 AMP). Running to God when trouble calls is the best thing we can do.

As Jehoshaphat and all of Judah cried to God, He answered and revealed to them the battle plan. God told them exactly where their enemies would be located but He also told them this: *You need not fight in this battle; take your positions, stand and witness the salvation of the Lord who is with you, O Judah and Jerusalem. Do not fear or be dismayed; tomorrow go out against them, for the Lord is with you'''* (2 Chronicles 20: 17 AMP). And what do you do at the battlefield when you do not have to do any fighting? You sing and dance in celebration of victory. King Jehoshaphat appointed singers to sing praises to God at the battlefield and as they sang, God's hidden hands fought for them. The result was that the enemies rose against each other helping to destroy themselves. What a victory!

God can do anything in any way because He is God and is not bound by human limitations or procedures. When we are faced with challenges, it is important that we do not simply swing into action based on what we think is the right thing to do under the particular circumstance. God does not work in only one particular way in a given situation all the time. The key thing is for us to trust God despite the situation. When we seek His guidance and direction, as did Jehoshaphat and Judah in this case, God will reveal to us exactly what we need to do. When we trust and obey fully, an outstanding victory is the only outcome.

Reflection
*Do you trust God enough to allow
Him guide you through all challenges?*

55

Haman's Evil Plot

*So they hanged Haman on the gallows
that he had prepared for Mordecai.
Then the king's anger subsided.*
(Esther 7: 10 AMP)

Haman was an Agagite and a prince in the court of King Ahasuerus
who reigned over a hundred and twenty-seven provinces which
stretched from the then India to Ethiopia. Haman was subsequently
promoted above the other princes in the palace, a position which
required the royal servants to bow before him as commanded by the
king. Before his promotion, a new queen, Esther, had recently been
crowned as a replacement to Queen Vashti who had publicly
dishonoured the king. Esther's selection as queen came through the
actions of her cousin Mordecai who worked as a servant at the palace.
Both Esther and Mordecai were Israelite captives living in exile, but
Esther's Jewish ancestry was not public knowledge at the time of her
crowning.

When Haman heard that Mordecai refused to bow before him, he was outraged, and as a result, chose to punish every Jew in the kingdom instead of only Mordecai, who had apparently dishonoured him. Consequently, Haman hatched a plot to destroy every Jew in the kingdom which, he succeeded in getting the king to endorse. When Mordecai became aware of this plot against himself and his people, he made a counterplan that involved Queen Esther, who called for praying and fasting by the Jews in the palace. Eventually, Esther presented her petition to her husband, the king, while revealing Haman's evil plot against herself and her people. This greatly infuriated the king. Eventually, the tables were turned, and Haman was hung on the gallows he had prepared for Mordecai and his estate passed on to the queen while the king also made a fresh decree empowering the Jews to defend themselves against any attacks based on Haman's earlier plot. Thus was Haman's evil plot thwarted.

Like Mordecai, we could encounter people who may dislike our guts, and as a result, plot our harm. They could be senior colleagues at work, family members in influential positions, neighbours who have connections in the corridors of power, or just anyone we may come across in life. We can be confident that when we look to God for deliverance in such situations, and do what He instructs us to do, God will orchestrate a turnaround that will make any such evil plot against us   backfire, as did Haman's plot against Mordecai and the Jews.

Reflection
Have you heard about any evil plots against you?
Do what Mordecai and Esther did.

56

Daniel In The Lion's Den

Then Daniel spoke to the king, "O king, live forever!
My God has sent His angel and has shut the mouths of the
lions so that they have not hurt me, because I was found innocent
before Him; and also before you, O king, I have committed no crime."
(Daniel 6: 21–22 AMP)

Daniel, who was an Israelite in captivity in Babylon, was appointed one of three presidents who presided over the hundred and twenty princes appointed to work in the kingdom under the reign of King Darius the Median, who defeated and succeeded King Belshazzar, the son of King Nebuchadnezzar. Due to his extraordinary nature, the king planned to set Daniel over the other presidents and princes, thus putting him in charge of the entire realm of the kingdom. Consequently, the other presidents and princes perhaps out of envy decided to set Daniel up.

Realising that the only way they could entrap Daniel was in connection to his devotion to his God, they came up with a plan to ban making any petitions to God, other gods, or man for a period of thirty days except such petitions as are made to the king alone. The intention here was to tempt Daniel to compromise on his daily supplications to God. Could it be that these conspirators suspected that Daniel's outstanding excellence and rapid progress was somehow linked to his devotion to his God? Their plan was to disconnect Daniel from his God who favoured and prospered him? Interestingly, although the king approved the request of the conspirators, imposing a penalty of death in the lion's den for non-compliance, Daniel nonetheless continued to present his supplications to God daily as before.

Daniel had fallen into their trap as they intended and had to be thrown into the lion's den. Their evil plan seems to have panned out! These conspirators, however, failed to reckon with the ability of the God of Daniel to rescue even from the lion's den. Perhaps they were unaware that Daniel's God was the creator of all things, including the lions in the king's den. Daniel's God shut the mouth of the lions and delivered him unscathed. Eventually, the same conspirators were thrown into the den, by order of the king who subsequently realised he had been manipulated, and were consumed.

Imagine if Daniel had compromised and failed to pray to God as he had always done. When we are tempted to compromise our faith or devotion to God, we have to carefully assess the real cost of such compromise. What do we stand to lose as a result? We should weigh what we might gain through compromising against what we will lose in return. We should also realise that when we take an uncompromising stand for God, He proves himself a faithful God.

Reflection
Consider what you might lose
if you compromised your stand for God.

57

Jabez Prayer

Jabez cried out to the God of Israel, saying,
"Oh that You would indeed bless me and enlarge my
border [property], and that Your hand would be with me,
and You would keep me from evil so that it does not hurt me!"
And God granted his request.
(1 Chronicles 4: 10 AMP)

Not much is known about the man Jabez based on the biblical account, except that he was a descendant of Judah, was more honourable than his brethren, and that his mother gave him his name because she gave birth to him in sorrow. Jabez, however, is well known as the man who prayed and got his request granted by God. With little information on his background, his name Jabez which in Hebrew means "he makes sorrowful" could suggest that Jabez had a sorrowful or painful beginning or past up until the time he made his prayer.

Jabez prayer was more a prayer for restoration or turnaround than a prayer for prosperity. He was not merely clamouring for wealth and riches but for a change of story. First, he asked that God would bless him indeed. The blessings of God are not exclusive to material things alone but include wholeness of being and soundness of mind. The blessing Jabez asked for, considering the story behind his name, would have included turning his painful and sorrowful past into a joyful and wholesome life and living. Jabez then asked for an enlarged territory. An enlarged territory, in addition to material property, could also imply an expansion of sphere of influence and impact including positively touching the lives of a greater multitude of people. Jabez went on to ask for God's presence, which alone is the greatest blessing. God's presence avails us of everything good including provisions and protection. Finally, Jabez asked to be kept from evil, denoting divine protection from everything bad.

Jabez prayer was therefore fully comprehensive taking into consideration both his material and spiritual needs. He sought more for God than merely what God could give him materially. Any wonder God granted his request?

Jabez prayer reveals that God's blessings and presence are also essential necessities in addition to material prosperity, such that in our supplications for a turnaround or change of story we must not fail to also, and firstly, ask for both. We should also ensure we pray to be kept from evil when things turn around for us and our lives change for the better.

Reflection
What do you want God to do for you?

58

Born To Be

"Before I formed you in the womb I knew you
[and approved of you as My chosen instrument],
And before you were born I consecrated you
[to Myself as My own];
I have appointed you as a prophet to the nations."
(Jeremiah 1: 5 AMP)

Our birth was not a random incident that occurred simply because our parents had intercourse, but instead, our conception and eventual birth took place as part of a deliberate plan. Similar to the deliberate planning behind creation, the conception and birth of every human was planned by God and for a reason. We were each born to be! To be the person God intended for us to be which in turn is based on the reason God intended for us to be in the first place.

As demonstrated at creation in the beginning, everything needed to help us realise our true identity (the person intended for us to be) and to accomplish our purpose here (the reason God planned our conception and birth) have all been provided for in advance of our conception. This provision is inherent in the divine ordinance occasioning our existence (which can be referred to as "the Word of our creation"). God's ordinance (Word) based on which we came into existence is all-inclusive. It contains everything that would or should happen to us, from the time of our birth to the time we die, including everything we need to actualise the life God had intended for us before causing us to be conceived in the womb.

It means then that instead of striving for "success", we ought to endeavour to realise our true identity and purpose, and live our lives driven by God's purpose for us in order to accomplish them. Living true to our identity and purpose will guarantee us access to the provisions contained and already available in the ordinance occasioning our existence. Otherwise, we risk engaging in fruitless endeavours, thereby also wasting our lives. Interestingly, if we did, we are bound to also achieve true success in the end, having accomplished the reason behind our existence.

Reflection
Who are you meant to be?
What are you here for?

59

※

God's Calling

Thou whom I have taken from the ends of the earth,
and called thee from the chief men thereof,
and said unto thee, Thou art my servant;
I have chosen thee, and not cast thee away.
(Isaiah 41: 9 KJV)

We all have the calling of God upon us, regardless of who we are, simply because He created us for a reason. The purpose behind our existence represents God's call or calling on our lives. It is very important to point this out, especially due to the common misconception that supposes God's calling relates only to such functions or offices connected with church or missionary activities. For the sake of clarification, whatever we are created to accomplish during our lifetime represents our calling and ministry; whether it relates to helping educate other people, establishing and running a business, providing care and support for the vulnerable, fighting for and advancing a positive cause, making an invention, or raising a family.

We, therefore, are all servants chosen by God as the right persons to accomplish particular tasks and missions. God's calling places onerous responsibility upon us, as no call of God is easy. Fortunately, God's calling is also God's enabling because He never requires us to fulfil a purpose or accomplish a mission for which He will not also equip and enable us to accomplish if we rely on Him. God's calling is not easy mainly because of the opposition waged against every of His purpose by the enemies of God and of humankind, represented by spiritual powers and principalities.

Adam, Noah, Abraham and Sarah, Jacob, Joseph, Moses, Daniel, Gideon, Esther, and Deborah are a few examples of people whose God's call upon their lives was enormous. Nonetheless, we learn from them how God is more than able to accomplish in and through us everything He has purposed for us regardless of the opposition we face as well as our human weaknesses and shortcomings. We only need to trust and obey God and we will definitely fulfil our calling.

Whatever our calling by God, we should realise that He will not expect from us more than He has equipped and will enable us for, meaning that we can and will accomplish our calling if we totally rely on God in the pursuit of His calling on us.

Reflection
What could God have called you for?

60

Is God Loving?

Your lovingkindness and graciousness,
O Lord, extend to the skies,
Your faithfulness [reaches] to the clouds.
(Psalms 36: 5 AMP)

"If God is loving, why has He allowed so much evil in the world?" is a question often asked by some people who doubt God's love due to the prevalence of evil in the world. Such as the many people living in abject poverty under impoverished conditions in different parts of the world, the rape and killing of very young innocent children, modern enslavement, slave and child labour, oppression and marginalisation of particular ethnicities locally and globally, various forms of injustice and unequal treatment of humans. Some of these practices and occurrences can make anyone wonder whether indeed God loves and cares for humanity.

God's love for humanity is unquestionable and attested to by creation itself which was founded and driven by love. Everything God created was certified good by God himself; we do good things out of love. God created humans last after creating everything else needed to make living enjoyable, and handed the world to us to take care of. How loving is that! Unarguably, the main problem of the world could be summarised in a single word—evil! Who is responsible for the evil in the world? We are. We became exposed to the knowledge of good and evil after the first humans disobeyed God and ate the forbidden fruit, having yielded to deception and temptation in the garden. The knowledge of evil meant that humans could now do evil, hence the many evil in the world.

Why doesn't God prevent people from doing evil or punish evildoers immediately after they commit an evil act? God is noble and faithful and does not throw His weight around just because He could. God has enabled us to choose between good and evil and allows us to freely exercise this choice which is not without consequences. Similarly, God does not instantly judge evil because He had appointed a time for this in the hope that we might redeem ourselves by turning from our wrong choices before judgement time. Perceived accurately, the foregoing demonstrates God's loving nature.

God intended for humanity to coexist in love, peace and harmony, which, if we did will make the world a far better place than it has been. God's love is why we are not individually destroyed because of our evil deeds and why the world has not been destroyed yet. God's love is the reason there is still hope left for us and the world because, in the end, God will make everything beautiful again as was the original intention behind creation.

Reflection
Do you believe God is loving?

61

Harvest Time

A time to be born and a time to die;
A time to plant and a time to uproot what is planted.
(Ecclesiastes 3: 2 AMP)

There is planting season and harvest season when our hard work is
rewarded, and we reap the fruits of our labour. Harvesting is
predicated on planting or sowing because we cannot reap when we
have failed to sow nor where we have not sowed. Likewise, in sowing,
we sow what we expect to reap and by how much. Where apple, for
instance, is the desired harvest, we ensure to plant apple seeds and not
the seeds of any other fruits. Where harvesting is intended for a
commercial purpose, for instance, we plant apple seeds on a relatively
larger scale than we would have if were planting for personal
consumption alone. Furthermore, for a good harvest, we also ensure to
plant at the right planting season for the particular crop in question
and under the right conditions, including soil type.

Suffice it to say that planting is not a carefree purposeless venture,
but instead one embarked upon with a predetermined goal in mind, a

harvest. Planting is, therefore a type of investment. Incidentally, life is also an investment. The seed in life's investment is the gift of life itself, represented by life, measured in time (seconds, hours, days, weeks, months, and years), as well as the various abilities and talents we are born with. The planting process is represented by how and what we do with these seeds, including the conversion of the opportunities we are blessed with. The harvest is represented by what we get out of life as a result of what and how we planted. Consequently, as an investment, we cannot afford to treat life with levity but instead, as we would other investment ventures which we undertake primarily for the purpose of making huge returns in the end. We should be intentional with respect to how we sow our life-seeds.

Since each life is created for a specific purpose, it becomes incumbent upon us to ensure that we invest our seeds of time, skills, abilities, talents, and labour rightly and timely in pursuing the fulfilment of the purpose behind our creation. Engaging in other ventures would be akin to planting seeds in the wrong soil or using our good soil to grow weeds or plants which are of no benefit to us. Only when we expend ourselves in the pursuit of the things meant for us, based on our purpose, can we be guaranteed a bountiful harvest when harvest time comes.

Every moment that we are alive represents a great opportunity to do what is needed to ensure we get a good harvest out of life.

Reflection
*Are you investing your life rightly
for an abundant harvest?*

62

One Day

And Pharaoh said unto Joseph, See,
I have set thee over all the land of Egypt.
And Pharaoh took off his ring from his hand,
and put it upon Joseph's hand,
and arrayed him in vestures of fine linen,
and put a gold chain about his neck.
(Genesis 41: 41–42 KJV)

One day begins a story and one day is also what it takes to change a story, no matter how good or bad. Conception occurs in a day and after several months of development in the womb, one day, a child is born. Death also occurs in a day. These all confirm that there is a time appointed for every season or occurrence in life. When the time appointed for each event comes, it happens, whether we are ready or not.

However, in some cases, we have to do the things required before certain things can be accomplished as ordained. For instance, for a child to be conceived, the parents have to first copulate. To reap, we have to first sow. The main point here, is to highlight that life is governed by time and timing is crucial in every aspiration or vision.

Joseph had a vision as a young boy, but a lot transpired between when he had his dreams and when they eventually became fulfilled. Following his dreams, he was hated by his older siblings, who subsequently sold him into slavery. He was enslaved for several years, and from slavery he was imprisoned, for several years. However, one night, when it seemed all hope was lost, Joseph went to sleep as an imprisoned and enslaved person but by the next morning, his story changed. Joseph became fully restored, and his dreams were finally fulfilled. His imprisonment, enslavement, joblessness, homelessness, singlehood all ended in a single day. The day appointed for the fulfilment of each! Job was another person who, after a prolonged series of vicissitudes, got restored starting one day.

We can take solace in the stories of Joseph and Job and be reassured that regardless of what we are going through, and for how long, one day is all it will take for things to turn around for us when we retain our trust in God, abiding in His will for us and doing only all He reveals to us to do. Let us, therefore, keep our hope alive and strong till that one day and not give up. Let us hold on and as it were, live for that day!

Reflection
Whatever it is, remember that your one day will come.

63

Living By Faith

"Look at the proud one,
His soul is not right within him,
But the righteous will live by his faith
[in the true God].
(Habakkuk 2: 4 AMP)

When God instructed Noah to build an ark which He would use to preserve Noah's household, and thus humanity, and all other animal species pending the destruction of the then world, Noah obeyed because he believed in God. Noah had faith in God that if God said it, He (God) would do it. Noah lived by faith. Similarly, when God called Abraham (then Abram) to depart from his ancestral homeland and from his people and proceed to a land that God will show him, Abraham obeyed simply because he believed in God. Abraham's life subsequently and his walk with God henceforth reveal a man who believed everything God told him. Abraham also lived by faith.

A quick review of biblical accounts also reveals that everyone through whom God accomplished great and impossible deeds, such as Joseph, Moses, Joshua, Gideon, Esther, Daniel, to name a few, all demonstrated rare faith in God. These also all lived by faith. Faith in this context is not just as defined in Hebrews 11, as the substance of things hoped for, the evidence of things not seen, but is simply a complete trust in God. Faith is to totally believe and rely on God in everything and at every time. Faith is to deliberately choose to seek God's guidance and direction in everything we do, always. Faith is to live driven only by God's directives regardless of the circumstance. In other words, faith is not simply a tool we employ only when we want to receive something from God, or answers to our prayers, but instead is a lifestyle.

True faith in God is a preferred attitude and chosen way of life. It is a choice we make to live a life driven by God—His will, purpose, and guidance—alone. This is what it means to live by faith. We need to choose to live by faith if we desire the best life, including being fulfilled at the end of our lives.

Reflection
Are you living by faith?

64

Almighty God

God has spoken once,
Twice I have heard this:
That power belongs to God.
(Psalms 62: 11 AMP)

God is almighty and omnipotent because power in its entirety belongs to Him. Power in this context refers to the ability or capacity to do something, anything. It is thus impossible to do anything except we have the power to do that thing. Now this power, to do anything at all, belongs entirely to God. It means then that except God empowers someone with the ability to do a particular thing, no one can do anything at all. At creation, God empowered everything created with the ability to do several things depending on the purpose of their creation. Thus light exists, and the sun, moon, and stars, for instance, shine and do everything else they are able to do. Likewise, humans are also able to do the things we are able to do because God has empowered us to do accordingly based on our creation.

God enables every power that is exercised by anything in existence. This includes the power exercised by spirit entities such as angels and those fallen angels commonly referred to as devils or demons. It is important to point out that the concept of a Devil, represented as a single fallen angel known as Lucifer, is flawed and misguided because it singles out an individual fallen angel as a leader of sorts who is wrongly positioned as God's rival and who possesses powers which are seemingly outside of God's control. The truth, however, is that the former archangel, Lucifer, who led a rebellion against God and was cast out of God's presence and heaven, as a result, is in no way an independent authority in relation to power and God. All fallen angels would rightly be described as devils following their fall, but they were all created by God. Thus the only power they have is as enabled by God during and in accordance to their creation, as applies to every other creation.

No power can be exercised by anything in existence, in the natural or spiritual, except that given by God. Such power thus belongs to God nonetheless, regardless of how it is exercised. The important message here is that God alone is almighty and thus alone is able to do all things. God is above the power He has enabled anything in existence, including the devils, and thus remains in absolute control over all of creation.

When we realise that God alone is almighty and that every power is subject to Him, then it becomes easier to fully trust in God at all times because we would then have understood not only is there anything God cannot do, but also nothing can be done except He allows it.

Reflection
Spend some moments reflecting
on the almightiness of God.

65

Ruth's Choice

But Ruth said,
"Do not urge me to leave you or to turn back from following you;
for where you go, I will go, and where you lodge, I will lodge.
Your people will be my people, and your God, my God.
Where you die, I will die, and there I will be buried.
May the Lord do the same to me [as He has done to you],
and more also, if anything but death separates me from you."
(Ruth 1: 16–17 AMP)

During the period when judges ruled Israel because a kingship was yet to be established, a certain man from Benjamin in Judah fled to Moab during a famine. His name was Elimelech. He migrated to Moab with his wife Naomi and two sons Mahlon and Chilion, who subsequently married Moabite women named Orpah and Ruth. Elimelech and his two sons died in Moab, leaving Naomi childless and widowed at old age in a foreign land. Following her misfortune, Naomi decided to return home to Judah.

Orpah and Ruth, Naomi's daughters-in-law, accompanied her in her homeward journey but along the way, she persuaded both ladies to return to their homeland in Moab where they could easily remarry. Although both ladies initially objected, Orpah subsequently conceded and returned home after Naomi drove home the fact that she had nothing to offer each lady. But Ruth chose to go with Naomi. The secret of Ruth's choice can be found in this phrase: *Your people will be my people, and your God, my God.* Despite the great misfortune that befell Naomi, Ruth realised that her mother-in-law had a greater God than the gods served by her people in Moab. Furthermore, Ruth did not judge the God of Naomi and her people Israel by the lot that befell Naomi, nor did she allow her misfortune to becloud her perception of God's greatness and faithfulness.

When Ruth arrived at Judah, with time and after a series of incidents, she eventually got remarried to a wealthy kinsman of Elimelech's called Boaz, with whom she had a son called Obed. Obed became the father of Jesse, who was the father of David, the second king of Israel. Who would've thought that a widow from Moab would   one day be the mother to the grandfather of a future king of Israel? As a result, Ruth is immortalised and remembered but her sister-in-law Orpah is forgotten as not much is known about what happened to her after she chose to return to Moab to pursue a better prospect.

When we are willing to forgo fame, fortune, and everything else in pursuit of God, what we stand to gain in return will significantly outweigh everything we were willing to give up. Our greatest pursuit should be God because when we have God, we have more than the whole world; we have everything God has.

Reflection
Will you choose God over everything else?

66

Jonah's Disobedience

Now the word of the LORD came unto Jonah the son of Amittai, saying,
Arise, go to Nineveh, that great city, and cry against it;
for their wickedness is come up before me.
But Jonah rose up to flee unto Tarshish from the presence of the LORD,
and went down to Joppa; and he found a ship going to Tarshish:
so he paid the fare thereof, and went down into it,
to go with them unto Tarshish from the presence of the LORD.
(Jonah 1: 1–3 KJV)

Jonah is popularly known as the prophet who disobeyed and tried to run away from God, however, unsuccessfully. God had instructed Jonah to go and proclaim judgement against the city of Nineveh due to the wickedness of the people in it, but he was reluctant and instead decided to run as far away from God as possible. Thinking about it, where could anyone run to and be free from God? Anyway, Jonah thought he could. So he set off in the opposite direction to Tarshish, having paid his fares, and boarded a ship.

God then sent a storm that almost wrecked the ship Jonah was travelling in. While the sailors desperately attempted to salvage the ship, including throwing away some cargo into the raging sea, the runaway prophet was below deck sleeping. When Jonah realised that his game was up and could no longer keep his secret to himself alone, he confessed everything. As the storm got fiercer Jonah suggested to the sailors to throw him into the sea but they didn't want to be responsible for the death of a prophet of God, and so they rowed even harder, hoping to escape the storm but to no avail because the storm's fierceness further increased leaving them with no choice than to do as Jonah had told them.

Perhaps Jonah had expected to drown upon being thrown into the sea (it is even possible he had preferred to die than go to Nineveh), but instead of drowning, he found himself in the belly of a great fish where he was miraculously kept alive for three days and night. God had rescued Jonah, who, having come back to his senses while in the fish's belly, repented and cried out to God. God heard Jonah and caused the fish to vomit him out on dry land, alive. When the word of God came a second time to Jonah to go to Nineveh as earlier instructed, he obeyed.

When we try to do what pleases us instead of what God wants us to do or live contrary to the way God requires us to, we put our lives in great danger.

Sometimes, like Jonah, we may wish to run away from the things we know God wants us to do, perhaps for one reason or another, but we must realise that it is impossible to run from God. Assuming we could, do we really think it is beneficial to us to run and hide from God? When we realise that God loves us dearly and truly and that all His plans for us are for our own good, we would desire nothing else but God's will for us.

Reflection
Are you in any way trying to run from God?
And why, if so?

67

⁂

Jonah's Anger

*But it greatly displeased Jonah
and he became angry.*
(Jonah 4: 1 AMP)

After Jonah initially disobeyed and tried to run away from God (having chosen to travel to Tarshish instead of Nineveh where God had sent him to go and proclaim judgement against the people living in the city, risking his own life in the process because of the fierce storm God sent against the ship in which he was travelling, and was thrown into the sea upon his suggestion, he was preserved by God in the belly of a great fish for three days and nights before subsequently repenting and crying out to God following which God made the fish to vomit him out on dry land, God gave him a second chance by instructing him to go again to Nineveh and fulfil the earlier instruction. This time, Jonah obeyed and travelled to Nineveh and did as told by God.

Jonah's mission was a huge success because the entire city of Nineveh believed his message, and as a result, everyone from the greatest to the least person repented while a fast was also proclaimed by the king of Nineveh forbidding anyone, including animals, from eating but instead to turn away from their wickedness and pray to God for forgiveness. God accepted their penitence, and instead of judgement, as initially intended, had compassion on them and averted the disaster He had planned to bring upon the people.

This made Jonah very angry, who only then revealed the reason he initially chose to disobey God and run to Tarshish instead of going to Nineveh. He knew that God was gracious and compassionate, slow to anger and great in lovingkindness, and quick to pardon sinners' transgressions. Jonah preferred instant judgement to divine mercy. He had forgotten that it was because of divine mercy that he did not drown on his way to Tarshish and that God also had compassion on him when he cried out from the fish's belly. Surprisingly, Jonah now requested God to take his life and angrily left the city to camp at an outpost outside the city where he sat and hoped that destruction would still befall the city. It was here that God taught him an invaluable lesson to the effect that every creation, particularly lives, are very valuable in God's sight and that He understands the weakness of humans regarding discerning and doing the right things.

We sometimes could behave as Jonah did and desire instant vengeance against those who have wronged or hurt us. Or we may even refuse to pray for those who persecute and oppress us or refuse to minister God's word and love to those we see indulging in wickedness and iniquity, preferring instead that God's judgement would be levelled against them. We also easily forget how we have wronged and hurt other people or may even have also persecuted and oppressed other people. Ironically, we might even be wishing God's vengeance upon those who have afflicted or are afflicting us while at the same time also afflicting other people, knowingly or unknowingly. We need to learn to be compassionate and merciful instead of vengeful and unforgiving.

Reflection

Are you vengeful or compassionate?

68

God's Presence

And the Lord said,
"My presence shall go with you, and I will give you rest
[by bringing you and the people into the promised land]."
And Moses said to Him, "If Your presence does not go
[with me], do not lead us up from here.
(Exodus 33: 14–15 AMP)

Nothing in the world could compare with God's presence, and nothing, absolutely nothing, could ever come anywhere close in ranking to God's presence. Moses understood the importance and necessity of God's presence; hence he pleaded with God not to require the people of Israel to take any further step in their journey through the wilderness to their Land of Promise, which God had promised to their father, Abraham. At the time Moses made this statement, the people of Israel were stuck on transit in the wilderness where they were exposed to all forms of danger, yet Moses preferred this danger and stagnation to any form of progress void of God's presence. Moses understood that outside of God's presence, nothing is worth doing.

What had happened was that God withdrew His presence from the people of Israel after they rebelled against Him and persuaded Aaron the priest to make an idol for them, in the form of a golden calf, while Moses was up on the mountain receiving the ten commandments from Him on their behalf. A physical demonstration of God's withdrawal was the removal of the Tabernacle of Congregation from the midst of the camp to a distant place outside the camp. It was in this tabernacle, now located outside the camp from the people that the interaction between God and Moses took place. God accepted Moses' intercession for the people, subsequently reassuring him that His presence will now go with the people as before. Only then was Moses willing to lead the people of Israel onwards on their journey to the land flowing with milk and honey.

God's presence is our most valuable asset, and no venture is worth being undertaken if it is void of His presence. God's presence guarantees light (thus clarity), right direction and guidance (thus success), provision, and blessings (thus prosperity, contentment, and fulfilment) but outside of God's presence is total darkness.

Reflection
What can you do without God's presence?

69

I Will Go Before You

"I will go before you and level the mountains;
I will shatter the doors of bronze
and cut through the bars of iron.
(Isaiah 45: 2 AMP)

God had anointed Cyrus, King of Persia, as a deliverer who would liberate Judah from Babylonian captivity and enable the rebuilding of Jerusalem. When God calls, He also empowers, and so God, through Isaiah the prophet reassures this king who was not an Israelite that He will assist him to accomplish the mission he was appointed for. God's assurance of Cyrus is detailed in Isaiah 45, including the promise that God will go before him to make his path plain by removing every obstacle on his way. Through God's assistance, Cyrus was able to accomplish his mission of enabling the rebuilding of Jerusalem.

Where God calls us to do anything, we can be sure that He has also made available everything we need to successfully complete the task, including His presence. However, it is up to us to ensure that we rightly appropriate God's provisions so as to avail ourselves of its contents. We must be careful not to rely on ourselves or to go ahead of God at any stage throughout the mission. Going before God would present us with many difficulties including mountainous obstacles which we cannot move by our strength. But when we allow God to go before us, He will level every crooked path,

Whenever we encounter obstacles on our path, we should first confirm that we are indeed on the right path; the one God wants us to take. Once we are certain that we are on the right path, we then need to present that obstacle to God and when we do, He will either remove it from our path, or guide us on how to overcome it. With God on our side and as our guide, there is nothing in the whole world able to prevent us from going forward.

Reflection
What mountain is before you
that God cannot remove?

70

Job's Friends

Now when Job's three friends heard of all this adversity
that had come upon him, each one came from his own place,
Eliphaz the Temanite, Bildad the Shuhite, and Zophar the Naamathite;
for they had made an appointment together to come
to sympathize with him and to comfort him.
(Job 2: 11 AMP)

Job was a very rare and unique personality with respect to his integrity and uprightness, and he had the equally very enviable position as the man whom God testified on his behalf as being blameless and unrivalled, and also made boast of his uprightness, reverence for God, and abhorrence of evil. Job was also a wealthy man. Ironically, due to his outstanding and admirable reputation, Job was subjected to a fiery trial that stripped him of everything he had, including his health, leaving only his integrity. When his three friends heard about his ordeal, they travelled from their respective locations to commiserate and comfort Job.

When they looked from a distance and did not recognise their friend, perhaps due to his disfigurement, they cried, tore their robes and threw dust over their heads. Their grief, sorrow, and pain was so great that for seven days, none uttered a word but instead sat in silence in solidarity with their suffering friend Job. Truer friendship could never be found. All was going according to plan till Job broke down under the weight of grief and lamented, bemoaning the day he was born. Afterwards, his friends took turns in chastising and remonstrating with Job, which devastated the suffering man even more. Sadly, instead of comforting their friend as was their original intention, Job's friends ended up causing him further distress, thereby failing in their well-intentioned mission.

We know Job's friends failed in their mission because God expressed His displeasure at their conduct and instructed them to offer sacrifices and get Job to intercede on their behalf in order to avert His wrath against their foolishness. Why did Job's friends fail in their mission? Job seems to offer an explanation here: *"For the despairing man there should be kindness from his friend; So that he does not abandon (turn away from) the fear of the Almighty* (Job 6: 14 AMP). What a suffering person needs from his friends is kindness, not accusations. Sometimes, like Job's friends, we also fail in our goodwill mission when we ignore kindness. When people are going through trials or affliction, what they need from us is lovingkindness. It is not for us to try unravelling the cause of their ordeal or to chastise them for being responsible for their circumstance. When we discern that something could be wrong, we are better off praying for them instead of trying to set them right while they are still in pain. We also must resist the temptation to take their actions or words personally because oftentimes, the words of a broken person are nothing more than a grief-stricken lament.

Reflection
What type of friend are you to the afflicted?

71

The Jealous Brother

Cain talked with Abel his brother [about what God had said].
And when they were [alone, working] in the field,
Cain attacked Abel his brother and killed him.
(Genesis 4: 8 AMP)

Adam and Eve, the first man and woman, had two sons named Cain and Abel. Cain was the older of the two brothers, but he wasn't entirely a good man. Abel, his younger brother, on the other hand, was favoured by God. When God accepted Abel's offering but rejected Cain's offering, Cain became angry and jealous of his younger brother. Driven by jealousy, Cain cornered Abel while working in the field and murdered him, thus becoming the first person on record to kill another human. Cain had committed an abomination and, as a result, was punished by God. Cain would henceforth be a fugitive and a vagabond and was cursed from the ground such that he would receive very little for his labour. What a price to pay for resentment!

Sibling rivalry is not uncommon or unusual in families but oftentimes is harmless. However, we must be very cautious not to allow ourselves to become overcome by such petty sentiments as are often present among siblings, family members, or even friends and colleagues, even when they appear harmless initially. It is better to deal with an offence immediately it happens than to allow it fester within us, thus making us angry, bitter, resentful, or vengeful. Great vices often start from small seeds which, when ignored, have sufficient room to grow. Such that a slight irritation could develop into anger, resentment, bitterness, and hate, and could culminate in murder. Or, a simple covetousness could grow into envy, jealousy, and acidic enmity ending with grave consequences. We, therefore, need to guard our hearts very carefully to prevent the wrong seeds from finding a nesting space in them where they are comfortable enough to grow and develop. Jealousy (as well as envy, anger, bitterness, resentment, hate, and enmity) hurts more the person harbouring it than the person it is directed against. It is akin to swallowing a deadly poison hoping that someone else would die as a result. It is futile, counterproductive, and could be very harmful to our health. Furthermore, it is one of the things God hates and for which He punishes offenders. We don't want to pitch ourselves against God for any reason let alone because of another person.

Reflection
Spend some moments reflecting on the danger of jealousy.

72

Rahab's Courage

Joshua the son of Nun sent two men as scouts secretly from Shittim,
saying, "Go, view the land, especially Jericho [the walled city]."
So they went and came to the house of a prostitute named Rahab,
and lodged there.
(Joshua 2: 1 AMP)

After the death of Moses, who had led the people of Israel from
Egypt through the wilderness for about forty years up to the verge of
their Promised Land in the region of Canaan, God commissioned
Joshua to take over the leadership of Israel. Joshua's first assignment
was to lead the people across the Jordan River to take possession of the
land on the other side. Consequently, Joshua decided to send spies into
the land of Jericho, which was heavily fortified with impregnable walls
all around the city. When the people of Jericho uncovered their
mission, the Israelite spies, two in number, made a run for it,
subsequently seeking refuge in the house of a prostitute named
Rahab, who hid them while diverting and redirecting their pursuers to

a different direction. Rahab's plan was successful, and the two spies returned home safely.

Rahab's actions reveal an act of powerful courage. What would've happened to her had she been caught assisting enemy spies? Rahab did what she did not merely out of kindness but also for other reasons including self-preservation. In return for helping them, Rahab made a deal with the two spies which would ensure that she and her household were spared when Jericho was eventually destroyed but it was what she revealed to the spies before striking this deal with them that gives some clue regarding the reason for her actions and courage. After recounting the great and mighty things God did for the Israelites on their journey, she states: *When we heard it, our hearts melted [in despair], and a [fighting] spirit no longer remained in any man because of you; for the Lord your God, He is God in heaven above and on earth beneath* (Joshua 2: 11 AMP). Therefore, Rahab's courage was rooted in her faith in God because she feared the God of Israel more than the wrath of the king of Jericho. Eventually, Rahab and her household were spared when Jericho fell and was destroyed by the Israelites.

Faith in God is precious and powerful because, through it, we can do things that ordinarily would have been impossible for us. When we reverence and trust in God more than we do our circumstances, strength will rise from within us to overcome such circumstances.

Reflection
What is your courage rooted in?

73

The Spies' Report

They reported to Moses and said,
"We went in to the land where you sent us;
and it certainly does flow with milk and honey,
and this is its fruit.
But the people who live in the land are strong,
and the cities are fortified (walled) and very large;
moreover, we saw there the descendants of Anak
[people of great stature and courage].
(Numbers 13: 27–28 AMP)

As the people of Israel led by Moses journeyed through the
wilderness from Egypt to their Promised Land in the Canaan
region, they camped in the Wilderness of Paran where God instructed
Moses to send twelve men, one each from every tribe of Israel, to go
and spy out the land of Canaan. Moses obeyed and sent the twelve
men as instructed. After forty days, the men returned and gave their
report having accomplished their mission.
All twelve spies confirmed that the land was indeed flowing with

milk and honey and had fruits in abundance, as God had told them. However, ten of the spies also presented a negative report which greatly distressed the people they were reporting to, causing them to rebel against Moses and Aaron. They focused on the size and strength of the enemy and how fortified their cities were. On the other hand, two of the spies, Caleb and Joshua were adamant that despite the strength of the enemy God was able to grant Israel victory. These two chose to focus on the might of their God.

Although factual to an extent, the negative report caused the people to rebel to the point of contemplating the appointment of a new leader who would take them back to Egypt, effectively denouncing God and their earlier deliverance from captivity. How sad! Due to this ingratitude and irreverence towards God, He decided that none of these people would enter the Promised Land except Caleb and Joshua. Instead, they would wander roundabout the wilderness for forty years till they were all dead, leaving only their children to inherit the land. The ten spies who brought the bad news died of a plague. What a price to pay for unbelief!

We therefore have to be careful about the type of report we present. The problem with the report of the ten spies is not that it was untrue but that it disrespected God by failing to acknowledge what God could do, as did the report of the remaining two spies. The problem is not in acknowledging a problem but when we exalt the problem above God, even if unintentionally. Whether it is a medical, financial, business, employment, or legal report, we have to be careful not to place its contents above the word of God. We have to ensure that we do not place any situation above God's ability to deliver us from it. We must acknowledge and honour God above every situation or circumstance because nothing is difficult for God.

Reflection
Whose report would you believe?

74

Moses

And the child grew, and she brought him to Pharaoh's daughter
and he became her son. And she named him Moses,
and said, "Because I drew him out of the water."
(Exodus 2: 10 AMP)

Moses easily fits the description "special child," "child of destiny,"
"favoured," or "privileged" as a result of the story of his birth and
childhood. He was born in Egypt to Israelite parents from the tribe
of Levi, at a time when the people of Israel had become captives in
that land having originally been invited and welcomed there as
migrants several years earlier. Israel's sojourn in Egypt was all part of
God's plan, which was revealed to Abraham their patriarch long before
it happened thus: *God said to Abram, "Know for sure that your descendants*
will be strangers [living temporarily] in a land (Egypt) that is not theirs,
where they will be enslaved and oppressed for four hundred years (Genesis
15: 13 AMP). God planned to bring Israel into Egypt for a period

before taking them out again to form a new nation in the land promised to Abraham.

Moses was part of that exodus plan. While Joseph was instrumental in bringing Israel into Egypt, Moses was to play a leading role in bringing Israel out of Egypt and into their own land. Hence he was preserved at birth and miraculously spared death. His story reveals the significant relationship between identity and purpose. Although born in Egypt and adopted by Pharaoh's daughter (making him an Egyptian prince, technically), his true identity was Israelite (a Hebrew) which is significantly linked to his purpose, to secure freedom for the people of Israel from the hands of Pharaoh and Egypt. Had Moses assumed a false identity; Egyptian, for instance, discovering and accomplishing his real purpose, the freedom of Israel would've been very difficult if not entirely impossible. Moses was born as a deliverer for his people. Discovering who his people were would require him to first discover who he truly was.

Like Moses, the reason God created us (purpose) is also intricately linked to the person God intends for us to be (identity). Fulfilment in life depends on a successful accomplishment of our purposes here. To discover our purpose, we must first discover and realise our true identity in who God created us to be. To uncover our identity, we have God to assist us because before He formed us in the womb, He knew us and why He created us.

Reflection
Do you know who and why you are?

75

✧

The Main Thing

Let us hear the conclusion of the whole matter:
Fear God, and keep his commandments:
for this is the whole duty of man.
(Ecclesiastes 12: 13 KJV)

Life is not without a reason or purpose, but instead, there is an objective behind existence generally as well as the existence of each person. Oftentimes, people ask or wonder if there is a specific meaning to life, if life means something or if there is a reason for life. In response, some people theorise that there is no particular meaning to life but instead that the meaning of life is whatever meaning you attach to it. And also that the purpose of life is whatever purpose we associate with life. While these assumptions may sound reasonable and logical, their greatest shortcoming is that they fail to acknowledge that life isn't a random occurrence but instead originated from a conscious decision and deliberate plan of the Creator, God.

God has a plan for the whole of creation and also specific plans for each person. Therefore, the true meaning of life can only be discovered with God's assistance since He is responsible for each life in existence. It is impossible to unlock the meaning and purpose of our lives if we left God out of our endeavours. We need to direct our quest for the meaning of life, particularly our individual lives, to God before we can get the right answer. God encoded our identity and purpose to constitute each of our lives. He alone can assist us in decoding our lives, including our identity and purpose, thus enabling us to find the meaning of our individual lives. Hence our whole duty here is to respect and revere our Maker, God, while also walking in total obedience to His instructions and commandments, including such instructions as are given to us on a specific and regular basis as we journey through life. Otherwise, a meaningless and unfilled life is the definite final outcome.

We don't want to live a meaningless life nor do we want to be left unfulfilled at the end of life here. Therefore, we must ensure that we acknowledge God in all our doings, revere Him, and also obey Him if we want our life and existence to be a successful one in the end. Life's meaning and purpose are found in God alone.

Reflection
Are you living a meaningful life?

76

Another Life

Many of those who sleep in the dust of the ground
will awake (resurrect), these to everlasting life,
but some to disgrace and everlasting contempt (abhorrence).
(Daniel 12: 2 AMP)

Death is a reality of life here and perhaps is the only certainty after birth. Death, however, isn't the end of existence because we are created as eternal beings by reason of our spirits which came from the eternal breadth of God, the Breadth of Life. Hence, after death, existence continues in another life. Although details regarding this other life after death are scanty (we don't know for sure how the afterlife is compared with life in the now), biblical evidence suggests that the afterlife would primarily consist of two main types of existence: Everlasting life and everlasting condemnation. Everlasting life has been visualised as a paradisiac existence with a glorified new body in a brand new and incorruptible world. On the other hand, Everlasting condemnation has also been visualised as existence in doom and a place of eternal torture and torment.

Fortunately, our future in the afterlife is literally in our own hands because our final destination is down to the choice we make. No one is predestined for everlasting life or everlasting condemnation but instead, how we live our life here and now would determine what side of eternity we end up. Putting it succinctly, living in obedience to God here will guarantee us a place in everlasting life while disobedience will result in everlasting condemnation. Trusting and obeying God happens to be a common theme running through the various devotionals contained in this book. Therefore, if we are to live according to the contents of everything we have read and learnt from this book, as well as God's direct instructions as contained in the Bible, in addition to the specific instructions and guidance God makes available to us as we journey through life, then we should stand a very good chance of making everlasting life our final destination after we depart from here at the end of our temporal existence here.

May we live here such that we would continue to live forever in everlasting life.

Reflection
Where would you spend eternity?

Other Books By Ziri Dafranchi

**OTHER BOOKS
BY
ZIRI DAFRANCHI**

MANNA
FOOD FOR THE SOUL
(VOLUME 1)

The first book in the MANNA series; the first devotional genre to combine poetic meditations and regular devotionals into digestible topics of faith, making it easier for you to choose and feast on what your soul craves.

www.hereditaspress.com

WILDERNESS FRUITS
ECLECTIC POEMS AND MUSINGS
(VOLUME 1)

The first book of the WILDERNESS FRUITS series; a novel combination of eclectic poems, traditional fables and short stories, and musings by the author with practical, applicable and inspirational encouragement. The fruits from a personal wilderness experience.

www.hereditaspress.com

WILDERNESS FRUITS
ECLECTIC POEMS AND MUSINGS
(VOLUME 2)

The second installment of the WILDERNESS FRUITS series; a novel combination of eclectic poems, traditional fables and short stories, and musings by the author with practical, applicable and inspirational encouragement. The fruits from a personal wilderness experience.

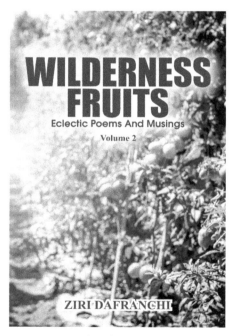

www.hereditaspress.com

LIFE
A MYSTERY SOLVED
(REVISED AND UPDATED)

The captivating philosophical nonfiction with answers to many of life's most controversial questions. Book One of the Trilogy of Truth.

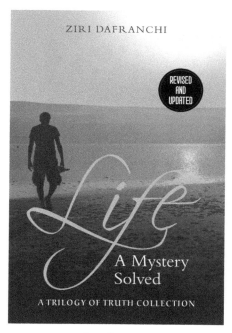

www.hereditaspress.com

BEING BLACK
REDISCOVERING A LOST IDENTITY

The deeply revealing truth about the hidden identity of some of today's Black people. Book Two of the Trilogy of Truth.

www.hereditaspress.com

PAGAN WORLD
DECEPTION AND FALSEHOOD IN RELIGION

The bold revelation about religion based on the present concept as a human rather than divine invention. Book Three of the Trilogy of Truth.

www.hereditaspress.com

Milton Keynes UK
Ingram Content Group UK Ltd.
UKHW010641040324
438885UK00001B/185